JUST COMPOSE YOURSELF

JUST COMPOSE YOURSELF

Finding Hope in Spilled Coffee

MONICA MOYER STOLTZFUS

Rise

An Imprint of Clear Fork Publishing

Just Compose Yourself: Finding Hope in Spilled Coffee

Summary: "Don't lose Hope."

The quote itself declares Hope's very existence. Then why, on those days when everything goes wrong in every possible way, does it seem as if Hope is nowhere to be found? Take a journey through the stories of Motherhood's messes and mistakes, freedoms and failures. You'll be surprised to see that Hope has never left us, rather it is us who must decide if we're bringing it along for the ride...

Rise - An Imprint of Clear Fork Publishing

P.O. Box 870 102 S. Swenson

Stamford, Texas 79553 (915) 209-0003

www.clearforkpublishing.com

Printed in the United States of America

Softcover ISBN - 978-1-950169-65-8

To my own Mother,

Thank you for walking beside me in these seasons of motherhood. Your faith and friendship have guided me and comforted me. I appreciate you, admire you, and most of all- love you.

CONTENTS

INTRODUCTION

A sweet friend once told me that if she was carrying the perfect purse and wearing the most stylish sunglasses, she felt she could conquer the world. I'd like to add to that - holding the perfect cup of coffee.

But Life just isn't that easy.

My sister thinks it's hysterical that I have Starbucks ordering anxiety. I sit in my car, hands sweating, and practice ordering before I enter. When I walk in, I start slightly mumbling to myself, knocking people with my perfect purse and sweating behind my stylish sunglasses. I end up stumbling over my rehearsed words every time. The professional orderers among me in line shake their heads and those seated at the tiny circle tables look up at me from their computers and cell phones with utter disapproval. However awkwardly it unfolds, I always leave with my perfect cup of coffee and I feel like I can, in fact, conquer the world.

Well, for the first sixty seconds. Until my perfect cup of coffee *spills*.

Does anyone else feel you might *look* the part, but as the day unfolds, your front is fading? The mascara is running; the deodorant has worn off, your perfectly styled hair is back in a messy bun. And the glasses, once perfectly perched atop your head, are now bearing down on the tip of your nose as you bend over, picking up the broken pieces and scrubbing the kitchen counter for the third time. It's all falling out of your hands.

This is me. 100%. My dear friends, my face should be on a poster for How to Spill the Most Liquids in one day. I'm not kidding. I once bobbled a full glass of red wine, tossing it in every direction and pretty much destroying the white pinstriped couch I begged my husband to let me buy months before. He now calls me "Wine Spilla, Couch Killa."

Ouch.

But I have learned something- spilling over is okay.

And Brokenness is a part of life. All our lives.

But Hope can be, too, if you grab hold of it.

I'd like to think hope is the glue that binds the fragile pieces back together again, helps to wipe up the messes we've made, and lights up the dark shadows cast by fears and failures.

One day, many years ago, a beautiful friend's brokenness had the last word. Her hope was not strong enough to hold the pieces of her life together. I was completely undone. She was bright and bold, a wonderful mother, a hard-working wife, and a dear friend. And while I was trudging through mother-hood with my young ones, overwhelmed and occasionally posting a picture on social media of exploding diapers or tripping over an upside-down bin of legos, my dear friend was also struggling. But her battle was being fought behind closed doors, completely unknown to many, including me.

I remember the last conversation I ever had with her. Filled with laughs and sighs . . .two mothers, friends, leaning upon each other just to make it through the day. I didn't know then what I know now, because it wasn't actually written or said in any of our conversations. But there was more: messages between the lines- where your heart does all the talking. I so deeply wish I had heard her whispers for help stashed amidst the questions of "How are you?" and answers of "I'm okay." Therein lies the quiet, blurry, gray, and too often lived-in world of "I wish I could tell you that *I'm not okay."* Here, my friends, is the setting and purpose of my book.

While the impetus to start my blog, Just Compose Yourself, was solely as a platform where I could easily share my home projects and musings with anyone who wanted to read, after the heartbreaking loss of my friend, the trajectory of my writing was drastically altered.

I pushed aside my projects and began sharing my own brokenness and shortcomings **composed** through epic blunders and little lessons learned along the way. I embarked on a spiritual and creative journey where it wasn't all DIY. It was more *D.I.G.-* Doing It with God. My goal? To truly **FIND HOPE** in **all** things, wrestle it to the ground and hold tight. Because I know it's there somewhere. In the darkest of days. In milestones and moments. Big and little.

And yes, even in that *spilled cup of coffee*.

ASSIGNMENT MOTHERHOOD

"Let all that you do be done with love." - 1 Corinthians 16:14

DEFINITION- MOTHER

Websters: " a woman in authority."

Mom definition: Therapist, law enforcer, professional boo boo kisser, live-in chef, occasional dog walker, teacher, pastor, part-time carpenter, shoe-finder, seamstress, permanent security blanket.

When I came to my editor with this idea, she was extraordinarily supportive. All throughout the writing process, she cheered me on and encouraged me to dive deep and "show more Monica." She was trying to pull the crazy stuff out of my head, bless her heart. But be warned- in my experience when opening up like this- we will either be best friends afterward or you will have put the book down and started vacuuming. So with her wise advice in mind, I'm rolling the dice and starting with a slew of confessions. It certainly does seem to break down any walls between writer and reader and makes it easier to dive into some deep stuff later on. So please bear with me as I shed some layers. It's not easy...

. . .

Confession 1: I battle daily with the need to make everyone in the world happy. Everyone. Even complete *strangers*. I really hope you like this book. Maybe you'll even love it. Or you'll think it will be pretty just sitting on your end table with a plant on top. And it will! Whatever you choose. I'm fine. Would you like some coffee while you read?

Confession 2: When I was around the age of fifteen and no longer in love with my blonde hair, I decided it should be dyed black. This insanely wise decision was based on the simple fact that there was an actress on TV who had beautiful, short, shiny, black hair. So, logically, I assumed that I too, would be beautiful with short, shiny, black hair. So I snuck out to the neighborhood CVS and after much agonizing over which of the 30+ boxes of smiling headshots to grab, I naturally selected the one who looked like she'd be the best babysitter. Well, my reasoning skills weren't quite as sharp as they should have been because when the dying debacle was complete, I had purple hair. Why? you may be asking. Because I panicked after leaving the color on for only three of the twenty minutes. I then completely lied and told my Dad that the shampoo did it. And he believed me. However, the next day when my mother returned from her business trip, *she* did not. And I've been slightly grounded ever since.

Confession 3: I was bumped out of the Girl Scouts as a child because I would not go door to door selling their cookies. Apparently, that's part of the deal. Alas, knocking on strangers' doors and potentially being told "No, go away" scared the dickens out of me. Actually, full disclosure- it still does. And now I'm sweating. Please refer to confession #1 for more details.

Confession 4: I am a PK (Preacher's Kid) and middle child. Phew, those two are quite the combo. From a very early age, I recited the words of the song *"Jesus Loves Me,"* but only in recent motherhood years have I discovered the true meaning when you sing "... we are weak but He is strong..."

Confession 5: I once saw a sign for a Neighborhood Leaf Collection and thought it was going to be a bunch of my neighbors, young and old, walking happily with ziploc bags, taking the time to observe and gather their most favorite of the fallen leaves scattered across our city's sidewalks and streets. I was very excited. However, I was sadly mistaken.

Confession 6: I was born four weeks early and immediately put on my back under the lights of an incubator, stark naked. My poor mother said I looked ridiculous, like a tiny little alien kicking non-stop while swatting flies. If you know about newborns you will understand how emotionally and physically detrimental this could be as they need to be swaddled, bonded "skin-to-skin" and have tiny little clothes put on at some point. I read an article once about how preemies who experience this while entering into the world have an innate yearning for blankets and hugging people and many times revert to a version of the fetal position while sleeping and sitting. This article is incredibly accurate. I am writing this while curled up like a pretzel on a dining room chair, wearing a fleece robe. In July. It is also probably and most definitely why I am obsessed with comfy throw pillows. So when my husband questions why I bought yet *another* one, now totaling around twenty-five and covering every inch of our home, we now know that it is one hundred percent out of my control. It's my baby subconscious.

> *I'm sorry. Can you hold on just a moment?*
> *It's my mom calling.*

Okay, I'm back. She called to tell me I'd better wrap up my list of confessions or she's going to put a plant on this book. Just kidding. She knows I'm far too fragile to hear something like that. She called to tell me she loves me.

But seriously, she's probably thinking I should wrap it up. And, at the huge risk of assuming you're still here, I will. Last confession, I promise.

Confession 7: Being a mother has been one of the hardest, loneliest, most confusing, and utterly exhausting things I have ever done. It has also been the most rewarding. And there lies the anomaly.

It's funny how painstaking it was to admit the first couple confessions and bare my soul like that, but then while typing the last, I came completely undone. This journey is not for the faint of heart. I've always considered myself slightly thin-skinned, not very tough at all. That's actually what's led me to the problems surrounding acceptance and people-pleasing! Being a mother has made me rethink everything I thought I knew about human existence and being tough. These tiny humans are needy and scrappy and strong-willed and energy-sucking and wild and wonderful and curious and loud and amazing and slightly needy. Wait. Did I already say that? I've always been on the emotional side, but this my friends, has turned me into a full-fledged hot mess.

I find it absolutely *insane* that you have to hand over your license and sign away your life to get a box of Advil Cold & Sinus at CVS, but the hospitals just GIVE us babies. We leave with them in our cars. And take them home. And have to try to keep them alive. Are we ready? Do we have the temperament for it? Are we perfectly planned and prepared for all things that will come our way? Nope. Not in the least. I don't care how many baby books you read or classes you take. Or even how cute that nursery is. (And those are some strong words coming from me...) But being a parent is pure insanity. And NO ONE, not even your closest friends and family, can truly prepare you for that.

You will never know what journey your children will take you on, either. Just when you feel like you've figured them out, they are in a new stage in life and their needs and feelings, likes and dislikes have completely changed. Without a single moment's notice. And where you once felt in control and in charge and sufficient, you now feel weak, ineffective, and useless. That is tough. I know wise ones around us try to tell us that we will be going through hills and valleys and that Motherhood/parenting is all about seasons. Well, I don't know about you, but I feel like there's been a cold, frostbiting, forever winter in my house that just won't go away.

My mornings are chaos, my afternoons are mayhem, and bedtime is a huge fail. I feel like I'm drowning, but yet swimming so very hard. Where am I going wrong? I feel like I've dedicated years to raising these little people with more love than yelling. And I've tried to model kindness, self-control, and gentleness. But they seem to be picking on the bad parts of me: my nit-picking, my obsessiveness for perfection, my exasperated "UGH" when things don't go my way.

But then there are those other days. When you catch them helping a friend, or packing a lunch without being asked, or even giving you a hug for no reason at all. Those are the times I want to remember. But as I write these words, I realize how unreal that is. We *will* remember it all-the hurt, chaos, and confusion. And the complete feeling of being so out of control that you might find yourself walking around your house clutching a Barbie shoe, a soup spoon, and some Scotch tape. And you have no idea where you picked them up or where they belong. I have screwed up, forgotten dates, turned in things late, missed parties, and disappointed those around me. Constantly.

But my children are loved.

At the end of the day, I may groan at heading up the stairs for the 14th time, for "one last kiss and hug," but I pray my heart softens as I think of those who will never be asked that request, either for the first time or, heartbreakingly, never again. So, I kiss them and hug them a little tighter. Yes, my friend, we are in the trenches. We wear our scars and we are fighting on what seems to be nothing but hills. The valleys are nowhere to be seen.

For now.

But, meanwhile, it doesn't matter how many times you and your children have fallen down in the day to day battles. I pray you have the strength to ***always*** get back up. Because that is how wars are won. I beg you to pour your love into your children day in and day out. They may roll their eyes at you, push you away, or even respond with silence. You may flop down on the couch overtired, unappreciated, and ready to give up.

But isn't that all proof that you are trying?

And at the end of the day, they will **know** they are loved.

And you, a ***job well done.***

MARATHONS FOR WALKERS

"I have fought the good fight, I have finished the race, I have kept the faith." -2 Timothy 4:7

DEFINITION- MARATHON

Websters: "a long distance race, something character-ized by great length or concentrated effort."

Mom definition: my day.

I went for a walk the other day and you know what I love?

Intersections. Not necessarily that you have to make a decision on where to go next. Lord knows I can't make a decision to save my life. Ask anyone who knows me. I'm like the scarecrow in The Wizard of Oz...I simply appreciate that it seems to give permission to pause. A much-needed pause. I tend to get super intimidated by long walks on long paths with no seeming end in sight. No place to make the appropriate, "I'm fine, really" break. I like to lean up against a tree, stop sign or even the occasional but randomly placed bench and huff and puff.

The other day was no exception. I was leaning up against a light-post and sucking down a bottle of water, when I heard some fast-paced steps behind me. I turn to see a bouncy jogger bounding up and down next to me. While I had chosen to stop and rest at the corner, this individual had kept her cardio going and continued to practice high-knees while the light stayed red. I thought I could TRY to look the part, she might be onto something, so I started a light bounce myself. Well, it only took 30 seconds of a few half bounces before the bottle of water sloshing inside my gut gave me jabbing cramps and I was now bent over heaving with strange sounds. The two of us could not have been more opposite. She gave me a weird look and darted across the road when the light changed to green whereas I looked like I needed an oxygen tank and a wheelchair to get me anywhere. And that my friend, is how I feel as a mother these days.

Back in high school when we were learning how to type, we practiced with a keyboard game that had a runner jumping over hurdles. When you succeeded at the home keys, or stated set of letters, your virtual runner soared into the air, breezing through the obstacles before him/ her. On the flip side, when you punched an incorrect key, your runner would fall and make this "oof" sound. It was funny. Actually, it was really funny. I once got in trouble for making him "oof" for 5 minutes straight.

I am feeling a bit like there's someone punching in the wrong keys these days. I see that hurdle coming, I feel like I'm almost ready for it, but then, next thing you know I'm lying flat with an "oof" sound.

With Teacher Appreciation and May's calendar exploding with dates to remember, and things to attend...I saw some serious hurdles approaching. But what I also realized was that when I SEE those hills and obstacles ahead, I tend to LOSE perspective quickly.

I heard in church yesterday that "*disaster can often occur when there is a loss of perspective*." My pastor went on to say that many airplane fatalities have resulted from pilots being unable to see the horizon ahead, and therefore, losing their perception of where they actually are in relation to the ground and sky. Inevitably ending in a crash...

Boom. What a visual. And it was exactly what I needed to hear.

When we are headed into the trenches, we often think we are *alone*, that the problems are *bigger than we can handle,* and that there is no *end in sight.* Sounding familiar to any parents? In my life, the term "Hills and Valleys" can appropriately describe my day to day. The battle JUST won can frequently yield little to no rewards on the next encounter with life. JUST when I have conquered something, had a little victory, succeeded in some small area- the very moment around the corner has a cartoon roadrunner waiting to toss an ACME anvil on me.

Last Monday:

Obstacle: Buy all teacher appreciation supplies in 4 hours.

Race prep: I had mapped out my route and memorized 4 different teacher surveys. I was ready.

Race route: Michael's, Target, Dollar Store, Home Depot (quickly for Adam), back to the Dollar Store, and finishing at Walmart.

Race results: NAILED IT... grabbed everything I needed to get through the first couple days and even sorted the supplies by teacher on the dining room table with cute, printed labels from Pinterest.

. . .

Ready for the children to help, I felt on top of the world. The feeling continued throughout the day, and even into the kids' bedtime. I flopped down on the couch, ready to reward myself with some Hallmark, when Autumn sauntered quietly into the room. She was holding a notebook entitled "My Days, My Dreams." She handed it to me and whispered, "I just wrote something new in here. Would you like to read it?" I love that she is my little writer, so I happily agreed. She snuggled in next to me and opened to this page.

"Mom comes for Writing on Monday (which today she forgot), Tuesday, Wednesday and Thursday. NOT Friday because she has Quinn, and Quinn is a giant handful."

Insert heartbreak. I looked at her and with instant tears, I apologized. She smiled a half-sleepy smile and hugged me again. She said it was okay and sauntered slowly back upstairs. What had I done? I thought I was the best mom in the world. THE WORLD. For a few hours at least... And then I saw this. I let her down. In her exact words, I "forgot." I was running around like a crazy woman, attempting to properly and Pinterest-worthily "Thank" every Tom & Sally. I "oofed." And I was lying flat.

And after an hour of ugly crying and Adam's repeated, "You are a good mom...", I went to bed, head pounding and heart-broken. I was certainly beginning to listen to the voices in my head saying "You can't" ...

But I woke up the next morning, (popped some Advil followed by strong coffee), gave Autumn an extra big hug, and told her I loved her. A lot. And she grabbed a Poptart and bounded off to school. Kids are crazy resilient.

I share this to help reiterate my own "full of faults" humanity and encourage yours. We are NOT PERFECT. We forget, we mess up, we fall flat. We "oof" all the time. But do you know what I've decided? **Your own children** are your biggest fans. To them, you are a superhero who is busy soaring high one moment and then falls flat the next. But you ALWAYS fly again.

Marathoners tell their families and friends to bring their A-game with signs and fog horns to the toughest part of the race. Why? **To keep them going**. To remind them how far they've come and how close they are to the end. To give them **Perspective.**

Who doesn't need a cheering squad? A pep rally? A hug? A smile? We all do. And life will not be without its **hills and valleys.** The tough times are inevitable. Especially as parents. Watching your children navigate through these dark places is downright dreadful. But please remind yourself and those you love-

*That you are never alone.

*The battles you face are not forever.

*It will be worth it all in the end.

Every tear, every pain, every hurdle, every heartbreak. He promises.

Go on & finish this race. 🩶

I'm not the marathon running type- in fact, I'm waiting on my **0.0** bumper sticker to come in. But look for me on the sidelines, at the closest intersection, huffing and puffing by the stop sign... **cheering you on**.

LOVE ACTUALLY

"Some days I amaze myself. Other days I put laundry in the oven." - Unknown

DEFINITION- LOVE

Websters: "an assurance of affection or devotion."

Mom definition: leaving your piping hot coffee in the microwave all day, while sprinting up to the school, bringing lunch and sneakers to an ungrateful spawn.

As I sit here and watch the overly stacked celebrities prance throughout the movie Valentine's Day, I have always been fascinated by the concept of an anti-love dinner party. It brings to light the idea that Valentine's Day- a day (months, really) dedicated to canoodling couples can be quite challenging to many. My thoughts then went to the upcoming Mother's Day. In lieu of this on-screen rebel party, may there be dinners and coffee dates dedicated to those who are not Mothers? If not, there should be.

This role or vocation as a Mother is TOUGH. There is no doubt about it... In fact, I stumbled upon a few quotes that summarize this quite well.

"MOM turned upside down spells WOW!"

"I live in a madhouse run by a tiny army that I made myself..."

"Mother: (muh*th-er*)-noun 1.) One person who does the work of twenty. For free."

"My kids are the reason I wake up each morning, the reason I breathe...and also why my hair is falling out, my house is a mess and I'm crazy."

While the reality of Motherhood is apparent, my heart has been with those who do not and will not celebrate this day. My mind wanders to those who fear this day and everything it stands for. Who, you ask?

Let us consider the woman who has lost her own Mother somewhere along the way. Maybe as a child or a teenager or even more recently. The woman who didn't get to share her wedding day, can't get that advice after a silly fight, or ever feel the warmth of a Mother's arms again.

How about the woman who has lost a child... maybe the child was a baby, in-utero even. Perhaps this woman had already planned a nursery, picked out a name, and planned how life would never be the same.

Or the woman who lost a child, but after the bonds of motherhood were set in. She held this child, sang to him, bathed him, clothed him. Sent him off to kindergarten with a tearful smile, kissed his boo-boos, and prayed over him each night ...

May we stop and consider the woman who is possibly suffering in silence, who dreads this day more than the rest. She, unable to ever conceive, holds her belly close as those around her celebrate births and babies. To her, this day is a reminder of what she cannot have.

I sat in bed last night and thought about this woman.

My thoughts ran to the day I watched in horror as the news unfolded in Sandy Hook. That night, my baby Mattie, like clockwork, startled me with her crazy screaming and fussing. I laid there, half asleep, feeling annoyed. Then it hit me. I tore off my sheets and ran frantically into the nursery. I scooped her up and I held her. I held her closer than I have ever held a child before in my life. And I cried. And cried. And cried.

I held her for all those Mothers who would never hold their children again. How they would do anything to hear one last cry or even a scream- or be woke up in the middle of the night because their child needed just one more hug, one more kiss, one more story. For them, there would never be one more of any of those things.

I write this not to take away from the joy of Mother's Day. I do write because I care. I care deeply for those who on these days, are in the trenches trying to keep their head above the water. It might be the working Mother of three, who hasn't seen her children in days and can't seem to muster enough energy to keep her marriage alive. It could be the woman who recently lost a child and walking into every store this weekend opens up wounds that have just started to heal. Or it may be the woman in the Starbucks, who seems disgruntled and crass, but there is more to her story...

So, I challenge my readers- on the Day of Mothers- may it be a day to spread Love. Love that has been given *to us* by our own Mothers- past or present. Give to the ones closest to you, and then possibly to a distant friend, a neighbor, or even a complete stranger. Imagine the possibilities...

MOMENT TO MOMENT

" Come to me all who are weary and heavy laden and I will give you rest." - Matthew 11:28

DEFINITION-JUGGLE

Websters: "to handle or deal with usually several things at one time so as to satisfy often competing requirements."

Mom definition: microwaving mac' n' cheese, slapping PB&J on bread, opening a pack of pudding with your teeth, and cleaning up a spill with a towel under your foot- all without skipping a beat.

Do you know what I would love? What I would **really** love? To not think. To not worry about what people will eat, or what clothes everyone will wear. Or library books or permission slips or homework or cleaning or dishes or appointments...I would love to not make any decisions for the day. The WHOLE day.

I'd like to recharge my MOM battery. And that involves a little shut down. If I'm an I-Phone, hypothetically, then I need to have all the apps that are constantly running-

CLOSED. If I'm a laptop, the programs all need that little mouse click on the upper right-hand corner- the X. Do you know what happens to something that's running too hard? It crashes. And I guess with technology, that's okay- we just replace it.

But you cannot replace YOU. Or anyone else, for that matter.

Would you like to know a mind-blowing fact that I learned recently? There will always be 24 hours in a day. **What?** I know it's not earth-shattering, but it was earth-shattering to me. I'll tell you why:

The people pleaser in me doesn't like to say no to anything. The mere thought of disappointing someone or possibly creating conflict makes my palms sweat. And to be one hundred percent honest, I think saying yes will make me more likeable. But it comes at a high cost. Believe me. The PTA needs a new chair for Teacher Appreciation? Yup, I'm your girl. Someone is sick and can't teach the kids in Sunday School? I've got you covered. Need help planning that baby shower? I'd love to... In fact, I'll host it and shop for everything. The list goes on and on...

As I continue to oblige, I imagine a color coded calendar of my life growing brighter and fuller. The fine lines in the squares are screaming. Yet, I convince myself that I can, in fact, do it all. And do it with flare. So I trudge on, the wheels in my head steadily turning on how to make the pieces fit. *I have a plan.* I can still make it to my sister's Zoom class if Quinn naps. I'll sneak a cookie or two from the dozen homemade ones as I'm heading to the church. I'll order everything for the baby shower on Amazon while blowing up the one hundred fifty assorted-sized balloons I need for school. Meanwhile...these new commitments and colors are bleeding and bending all over the calendar as I blindly scribble over and erase what once existed in that original blank space. *Time.*

But don't worry. It's all fine. **Really.** I'm *fine.*

Can anyone relate? If not– can I get your number? I'd love to know your secrets.

If yes– hold fast. You are not meant to feel this way. We are not meant to be superheroes. We are not perfect. We try to juggle...we think we are amazing jugglers, actually. But there is only one of you and you cannot do it all. You may try– as I do, many, MANY times. But inevitably, there is trouble ahead. Either a manual shutdown needs to occur– or a crash is coming. You know what my crash was?

Pain. And not from any huge trauma or accident. It came from being ME. I don't sleep much, and, apparently, chocolate-covered almonds mixed with coffee aren't all that nutritious. I'm always bending over and moving toys from one place to another, carrying children throwing tantrums from totally quiet places, and proving to the world that I can and WILL balance all my 15 grocery bags on one arm while pushing a stroller and holding an umbrella. (I'm seeing a little Cat in the Hat sketch in my head.)

But, alas, due to such adventures in motherhood, I am in some sort of minor to major discomfort 70% of the day. Shoulders, back, neck, chest, arms. My affliction got so severe that I couldn't lift my right arm past my shoulder. It is incredibly difficult to make a balloon arch with that range of motion. So, I sought out the aid and advice of a physical therapist, who recommended I slow down. And do less. Do you know what I rebutted? "This is Teacher Appreciation Week... so, I can't really rest just yet. Sorry."

This kind man went on to tell me that I am only harming myself if I don't seriously stop running around. He proceeded to wrap me up in horrible, yucky sports tape and told me I had to wear it for a whole week. (In tank top season!) After a loud groaning noise, I politely inquired as to whether this tape came in any other nicer colors. He half smiled and told me our session was over. As he held the door for me and my mess on the way out of the office, he quietly commented, "Try not carrying all that heavy stuff around all day...okay?" And he could have just been speaking of how I had Quinn flailing on my hip or the absurd weight of my perfect purse propped on my taped-up shoulder, but his gentle smile and the way he said it made me think it meant something a little *more*.

Friends, I am not good at this. In fact, I would earn a big "F" in time management, self-control, and declining events. But, I *am* deciding to start asking for *help*. From my friends, my family, and my Heavenly Father. I can't do it alone. And I'm not supposed to. So-back to my wish. I'm wishing to NOT do it all, because I certainly need the practice. I'm beginning to believe it's not selfish, or self-centered, or even a sign of weakness to put yourself first every once in a while.

24 hours. 1, 440 minutes. And dozens of opportunities to pry open those tired hands of ours, lift them upwards and take a load off. The best part? A moment of surrender only really takes a moment...

SUMMERTIME & GROWING PAINS

"We cannot direct the wind, but we can adjust the sails." - Dolly Parton

DEFINITION- GROWING PAINS

Websters: "the stresses and strains attending a new project or development."

Mom definition: accepting the fact that you will have more Pinterest fails than photos.

It's the heat of the summer and something pretty obvious has just hit me. My kids don't really like each other. Well, not at this moment... and I have spent the past week pretty upset about it. But then, upon slight reflection of my own childhood, it occurred to me that this is pretty normal for siblings.

My kids and I for that matter, have been on a totally different schedule for the last nine months- a school schedule. One that is allotted for individual time within the safe zones of classrooms, peers, projects, and priorities. Now, we are navigating through the waters of Summer- together. And that seems to be the pinnacle of this quest. We are ALL TOGETHER.

Now, for some reason, I thought this would be a seamless, smooth transition. But alas, there has been more hair pulling, tattling, tantrums, and time-outs than the past nine months combined. Enter the feeling of frustration and failure....

It made me think back to my own childhood when my younger brother, older sister, and I would be asked to "play nicely" together. Now, I have decided that many of us look back on our childhood with somewhat rose colored glasses- which gives me hope for my own children. But if I really remember what actually happened in those moments, I'll notice that we weren't all that different.

A quick example: My sister and I shared a room for most of our youth and one day she decided we'd "play nicely" ... in a **_new and improved_** layout that included duct taped perimeters on the bedroom carpet. She had access to the bathroom, dolls, toys, books, and, of course, the bedroom door. I had the closet. She stated that these were the new play areas and to have fun. Then she left, out the door, that I couldn't touch. Or the times when my younger brother asked us to go outside to play basketball with him. And our answer was always, "We'll be right out".

Now, you may ask what's wrong with that? Here's the thing... we never went out. But don't worry. As a result, he sharpened his solo "HORSE" playing skills, learned a ton of patience, and he eventually whipped up on the neighbors down the road. _He's fine._ I promise.

My point is this: summer can be tough. On everyone. When you throw everyone into the mix and hope everyone just politely and calmly gets along, it might just be the opposite- a teensy bit of chaos-until things can work themselves out. Like when your kids completely forget how to put away things, clean up things, not break things, and how to close the fridge?????

Ah, yes- ***growing pains:*** "...the stresses and strains attending a new project or development...and medically dull, pains of varying degree in the limbs during childhood and adolescence, often popularly associated with the process of growing" according to Merriam Webster Online. We all get 'em. But how can we survive them? I am far from a seasoned professional, but I have a few simple ***suggestions*** based on what is percolating over here at our place.

Suggestion 1: **Throw out all the expectations you had.**

Sometimes your worst enemy can be unreal expectations- and this is coming from a serial Hallmark enthusiast. I find that I get utterly frustrated when things don't go as "planned." But I am coming to realize that some of the best plans are actually completely *un*planned.

Suggestion 2: **Don't compare your day/ week / month / season to anyone else.**

This one is a true struggle for me. It's not just social media. It's everything. Should my kids be in camp? Are they supposed to be eating popsicles instead of breakfast? Should they go see the new movie in the theater? The neighbors just went on a family bike ride through four different state parks. Why can't we? I mean, I've taken approximately one spin class at the gym last year and Quinn just got her training wheels off, so it's obviously a hard "yes" from us.

Just kidding.

Go your own way. Your family is unique. It has its own needs and wants. Don't worry about what everyone else is doing this summer. Gather ideas, "like" people's photos, but don't get down in the dumps because you aren't keeping up with the Joneses. No one is, really.

Suggestion 3: **Stay *focused* but *flexible*.**

Similarly to suggestion 1, it's good to have ideas but helpful to be open to new ones. Kids absolutely thrive on structure- some more than others. I am certainly not suggesting you just coast through Summer like a California surfer, but it's also the time of year to push dinner back an hour or two if there's some serious pool fun going on. Or bust out the pillows and blankets for a movie day (yes- a whole day!) if everyone is cranky... which leads me to #4...

Suggestion 4: **Take breaks within your break. *Seriously*.**

Remember that distance makes the heart grow fonder? Well, that's pretty "tried-and-true." The same can be for a family that is suddenly spending loads of time together. The way we have survived the past couple days is by a *QUIET HOUR*. In separate places. They need it. **I NEED IT**. I'm catching up on laundry, doing a 15-minute workout video, writing! or even catching some ZZZ's myself... and it's just 60 minutes. I promise it's a glorious time to reboot. For everyone.

Suggestion 5: **Love 'em while you got 'em.**

I'm not going to hit you with statistics of how you only have 17 summers with your kids before they're off and gone... but I will leave you with this thought. I fell asleep the other night thinking about how my girls are getting to the ages where for much of the day, I find myself needed less and less. They can fix their own breakfast now, dress themselves, reach things, brush hair, play games, even swim at the pool. But although they don't always **need** me... they still **want** me. I know that this will someday change, and for my oldest, I fear it is coming sooner than I'd like. So, amidst the chaos and calamities, flaws and failures of my mothering, somehow, they are still reaching out. For my hand, for my help, for my **heart.** I'll take it.

So maybe the differences between painful limbs and pains in life aren't all that far apart. They both hurt while you are going through them, but they bring renewed strength and reach in the end. It just requires working through the aches and pains and a little **leaning in...**

INTERMISSION

Intro to the Quinn Chronicles

Have you ever seen the quote, "All I'll ever need to know, I learned in Kindergarten?" Well, friends, all *I* ever needed to know I've learned from *Quinn*.

Never in my wildest dreams did I imagine a tiny human could be so much work. I found a picture I posted way back where Quinn is sitting in a box and I've captioned it "this package *did not* come with instructions." That pretty much sums it up. She is wild and wonderful. But for most of her sweet little life, the wild part has slightly dominated. People warned me that when we went from two children to three- that we would inevitably lose our zone defense. Our one-on-one adult to kid ratio would now be a man down. I most certainly understand that. But no one told me the new addition would never, ever let my heels hit the floor.

Throughout this book, I will be periodically pausing to bring you lessons learned from my *escapades with Quinn*. "**Quinn Chronicles**" I like to call them. Before her, I was living life. But now with her by my side, I'm living life to its *fullest*. And I pray, I'm a tad wiser...

IT'S A NUMBERS GAME: HOLDING ON AGAINST THE ODDS

"Being happy doesn't mean everything's perfect. It means you've decided to look beyond the imperfections." - Unknown

DEFINITION- FLAWLESS

Websters: "having no imperfection or defects."

Mom definition: what my tired, wrinkly, sunspotted skin will never be. No matter how much makeup I put on.

"As far as the laws of mathematics refer to reality, they are not certain, and as far as they are certain, they do not refer to reality."-Albert Einstein

"Mathematics is written for mathematicians."– Nicolaus Copernicus

1, 2,3, 4, 5, 6, 7, 50+,

No, these are not the next winning lotto numbers- although- I might just give it a try!

These are simple numbers pertaining to my wonderfully chaotic life:

1–beautiful, loving Heavenly Father keeping me centered and alive

2 – times a week that I wash, blow-dry & straighten my hair & put on makeup.

3– times I've fallen down our front steps. Walk much?

4– books I've read since becoming a mother years ago ... Eeek!

5-seconds it takes my 3 little blessings to destroy the house.

6-minutes it actually takes to unload the dishwasher... Then whhhyyyyy do I dread it so much??

7– years it took my husband to propose.

50+ letters of rejection from editors & literary agents.

Ouch. The last one stings a little. Almost a tie with the **7** years thing... I mean, come on! Really?? Back to the writing... Fun fact? I don't usually share that number (with anyone outside my little family circle). Just checking. Are we in the trust tree? With the nest...? Still with me? No judgement, remember?

Okay. I'll continue.

Why didn't I share this part of me long ago when I took the plunge to pursue my passion? Numbers. I knew the statistics of a first-time writer "making it big" in the publishing world. I knew the odds were against me. And I did not want to be judged for all my failures. **50+**to be exact. I'd rather be known for all my achievements! (Did I mention I make beautiful wreaths?)

But it occurred to me that there were most certainly people out in the world who have failed at something (or many somethings!) at some point. And there are those who brushed themselves off & rose above it. Since then, I opted to view it as **50+** times I chose **NOT** to give up.

I like to picture **two** different dinner parties going on- **one** next door to the other. At the first, people gathered, engaged in serious conversations involving their latest and greatest feats of accomplishments, each **one** more determined than the other to outshine and one up the guests. There is a lot of sweating. At the second home, a loud rally, popping with stories of recent screw-ups, epic blunders, and famous face-plants- erupting with waves of laughter and high fives. There is even more sweating, but the good kind. In my ever-advancing adventure to redefine reality, I choose the latter shindig. Anyone with me?

So, it is with those brave "goofed" souls in mind, that I share - slightly timid- but with a new sense of pride. Because it's who I am. I am a writer. I did try to stop once- after a pretty big "no" came waffling in. It hurt. A lot. I decided to take a break. So, I stuck my journal deep down in a box and shoved it way up in the closet. Did it work? Ha- I just scribbled notes & ideas on the back of shopping receipts & school flyers. Even then, I still hesitated to send my work back out again, rejection still ringing in my ears and heart. But, in response to a prompting- a quiet voice -plus the incredible encourage-ment of my husband, I started typing up my very first blog post.

The completed piece was barely a hundred words and some-thing about eating more ice cream during the month of August... real life changing stuff. I honestly couldn't even tell you what I wrote. But what I do remember, quite vividly, was the moment a button popped up on my computer screen with the words "Publish now?" I completely froze. My newfound confidence came to a screeching halt. Hands-pouring with sweat. Publish? Like my stuff is going to be out there? For everyone to read? Or ignore? What if they *hate* it? What if they *don't* hate it? Isn't this what I've always wanted?

It's who I am. Then what on earth *am* I waiting for? Half of me was yelling, "HIT THE BUTTON, WOMAN!" while the other half was hiding in the corner with her hands over her eyes, begging, "DON'T DO IT!"

I hit the button.

Exactly ten days later, this unique platform of virtual blank paper served as the avenue for the tears emptying from my breaking heart. I had suddenly lost one of my closest childhood friends and I could not comprehend it or really speak without coming undone. But I could *write*. With each word I typed, I grew closer and closer to a place of healing. A tiny light inside of me brightened. It became my medicine, my mantra through the pain. After a prayerful pause, I hit that button again. Only this time I felt His gentle hands guiding mine as I set my sorrowful story free.

You see, we each have special gifts. They don't always come in the splendidly wrapped package we expect or hope for. Sometimes it's disguised or might even be so covered in our daily chaos that there's a little dust. It's completely up to you and me what we do with this unique present. My prayer for you? Own it. Once you start shining, there's no stopping the possibilities. The world needs you. And don't worry about being perfect or flawless: it's very boring and (spoiler alert) there's no such thing. I promise.

I leave you with this happy equation:

1 hurting world + **1** inspired individual who fights to make a change and *DOES* = a beautiful story **2** tell.

And that, folks, is just *simple Math*.

THE BARE NECESSITIES...THE SIMPLE BARE NECESSITIES

"Start by doing what is necessary, then what is possible; and suddenly you are doing the impossible." - St. Francis of Assisi

DEFINITION- NECESSITY

Websters: " the quality or state of being necessary, an urgent need or desire."

Mom definition: Jesus and strong coffee.

"Look for the bare necessities

The simple bare necessities

Forget about your worries and your strife

And don't spend your time lookin' around

For something you want that can't be found

When you find out you can live without it

And go along not thinkin' about it

I'll tell you something true

The bare necessities of life will come to you"

Original song written by Tony Bennett

Recently, my family and I chose the newest version of Disney's "Jungle Book" to watch on our weekly movie night. A true highlight for me was familiarizing myself with the great songs from long ago. I found myself singing Baloo's famous "Bare Necessities," all weekend long. The song begins and ends with the earlier catchy chorus.

Thank you, Tony & Baloo for weighing in on a pertinent topic. Question: Do you think you have a lot on your plate? Second question: Who put all that on your plate? If there is any slight, *eensy, teensy, weensy* chance that you might answer "Me," then continue reading. If you answered "Someone Else, then go ahead and slap them in the face. Just kidding. Keep reading, too. You need it. You just contemplated slapping someone.

As a stay-at-home mom, there is an innate need to fill my days with stuff. What kind of stuff? Well, things that make me look and feel like I'm doing my children and therefore, the world (of course), a great service. But there is a huge flaw in this mindset. ***I can't do it all.*** Not because I lack the skills for such endeavors. It simply comes down to necessity.

Why do we run and sign up for every opportunity to "help out?" I want to say it's because the human race is extremely generous and cannot sleep without giving 100% to each other. Sadly, this is false. I believe we are trying simply too hard to fill our days. And with what?

If you are sitting in a room full of people, and a clipboard goes around asking for volunteers for ____ (fill in the blank), a daunting number of these anonymous individuals will sign up. And not necessarily because they want to help. Admit it: it just "looks good" when we try. But here's a memo: trying doesn't always cut it. Statistically, the numbers drop as an event gets closer and as the leader reaches out to the numerous, once-cheerful helpers. Somehow, life has gotten in the way. And that *is* the simple truth.

Now, what does this all have to do with *you*? You do not have to fill your minutes, hours, days, and years with stuff. Despite your natural inclination, you are not being judged on how "much" you accomplish in a day's time. I'd like to believe it is more about quality and *how* you spend your time. If you have done **one** thing and done it well, I think you should be extremely proud.

Do you remember the slogan, "KISS: Keep It Simple, Stupid?" I sure do. It was written on a huge computer banner in one of my high school math classes. According to Wikapedia, it was a design principal noted by the U.S. Navy in 1960. Who knew this funny acronym would stick with me? "The KISS principle states that most systems work best if they are kept simple rather than made complicated: therefore, simplicity should be a key goal in design and unnecessary complexity should be avoided." If only I could live out this principal. Apparently, I tend to choose "unnecessary complexity." Repeatedly.

A quick personal example: Back when my oldest daughter went off to Kindergarten- I threw myself in (after all, this was my pre-mommy life for ten years!) and despite my better judgement, signed up for EVERYTHING. I thought it might help me be the best "Kindergarten mom" I could possibly be. Spoiler alert- I was wrong. The other day, the teacher reached out to me, (slightly assuming I'm available at the last minute, or wait... I think I told her that I am...) and asked if I wanted to help the class make ant hats. I, of course, agreed immediately, and turned an already tightly packed day into a full-fledged frenzy. Eek. Begin the face slapping. I'll spare you the long-winded details, but I'll paint this image.

While I was busy stapling and gluing ant thoraxes and abdomens, my darling Quinn has decided to pitch her socks and shoes, unclick her stroller brake, shimmy down the hallway behind me (while still strapped in, somehow), steadily crushing goldfish crackers and destroying any and every piece of beautiful wall art created by the young learners I was trying to aid. In hindsight- I really shouldn't have gone to help. I KNOW what Quinn is capable of. She is the biggest handful of a child on the planet. Honestly, she is. I love her, but she's a hot mess. Why on earth did I think she was going to act any differently for this one time? Didn't she get the extreme importance of my volunteering and my stay-at-home-mom self-worth? She did not and chances are neither will your children or even other people in your life.

My trying wasn't exactly enough. Certainly, no brownie points awarded. I'm not saying the teacher wasn't grateful. Quite the contrary, I received a very sweet email thanking me later that day. But what I figured I'd read was, "Thank you for coming, but please don't come back...ever." I am almost 100% sure that the chaos I ensued on her and, sadly, the other children- as they received their tattered artwork courtesy of Quinny Poo, far outweighed the "helpfulness" of my being there. Lesson learned. And one solid point for the hubby. (He MAY have warned me the day would go this way.) I urge you, please don't follow in my footsteps.

If you manage to wake up, dress yourself, and care for those around you, you are accomplishing A LOT. More than you know. Autumn may remember that I came to school that day, and she may even ask me to do it again. But she will not determine how much she loves me, or what kind of a mother

I am if I take a step back and politely decline the invitation. I'm hoping it makes me a smarter, more loving, more well-balanced mom. <u>Knowing your limitations</u> is a huge step in the right direction. The direction that seems to lead to a happier, uncomplicated life. And I dare to say, we can *certainly* do with a few less "worries & strife" to juggle.

I encourage you all to dial down your habitual "**Yes**" every once in a while; at least to anything that's not a bare necessity. (We are in this together!) You won't let anyone down or do anyone a disservice. You will be doing ***yourself*** a favor. And *you* are worth that. Now, that's something to check off on a list! I bet you will actually enjoy the freedom, peace, and simplicity it brings. You might even have a minute to just breathe and actually drink your coffee. *While it's still hot.* And who can say "**No**" to that?

THE NEXT BEST THING

"My To Do List- 1) Count my blessings 2) Be creative 3) Spread
kindness 4)Let go of what I can't control 5) Take chances 6)
Enjoy the little things 7) Smile more 8) Give it my all 9)Breathe"
- Unknown

DEFINITION-VICTORY

**Websters: *"achievement of mastery or success in a
struggle or endeavor against odds or difficulties."***

*Mom definition: when all the little socks actually have a match
coming out of the dryer.*

To-do lists. I have a love-hate relationship with them. I love
writing things down on paper (total writing nerd alert, I
know). I hate how long the list can look. I love crossing
things off. I hate when I add something. I love feeling accom-
plished and organized. I hate feeling like a failure and out of
control. In short: I love when I *can*. I hate when I *can't*.

Did you know there are 18 different "to-do list" apps? One
such app has a great mission statement... a promise of
"feeling calm and in control." But, alas, would a loud ding sent
by your ever-present phone actually help the situation or
hinder it? Do lists really create peace of mind?

Did you know that Benjamin Franklin is often considered the "grandfather of lists"? In fact, he was extremely list-oriented. Below is a picture of one such daily list.

(History buffs... get ready)

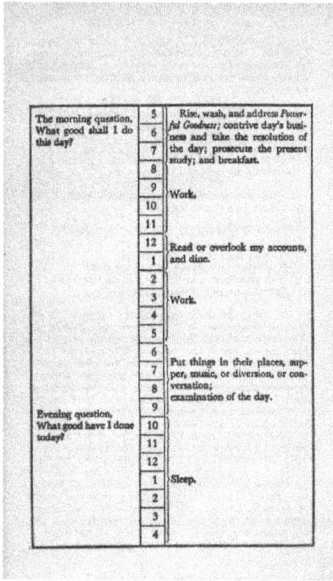

The morning question, What good shall I do this day?	5	Rise, wash, and address *Powerful Goodness*; contrive day's business and take the resolution of the day; prosecute the present study; and breakfast.
	6	
	7	
	8	
	9	Work.
	10	
	11	
	12	Read or overlook my accounts, and dine.
	1	
	2	
	3	Work.
	4	
	5	
	6	Put things in their places, supper, music, or diversion, or conversation; examination of the day.
	7	
	8	
	9	
Evening question, What good have I done today?	10	
	11	
	12	
	1	Sleep.
	2	
	3	
	4	

～

Notice the questions that he posed- Morning question: "What good shall I do today?" Evening question: "What good have I done this day?" There's breakfast, work, dinner, even "put things in their places" & "conversation" on Dear Ol' Ben's list. I cannot help but focus on *his* focus.

"Good."

And a conscious effort to embark and actually do it each and every morning, combined with an evaluation of the "goodness" of his day. Incredibly inspiring. Here's another idea.

Why couldn't we just pray over our lists and then Do The Next Best Thing? Would that be so wrong?

How about **emphasizing** the little victories of life (you found a missing sock!) and **de-emphasizing** the anxieties of the looming "un-done"? I will share a personal example. A few years back, I joined TWITTER. It has been invaluable.

The connections I have made with the writing world have been incredible. Alas, since then, I have noticed that I'm slightly distracted by the productivity of my pencil-clad comrades and more aware of my own proverbial treading water.

How much are they working??? She was up at 5 am and writing? She wrote 3 manuscripts already this month. Jeesh. I didn't write today or this week. However, I took care of my kids. Also, I ate breakfast! And changed out of my yoga pants!!! Oh, wait. No, I didn't. Crap! I'm hungry. And where's Quinn????

But you know what I **did**? I changed 2 sentences in one of my stories. Two. And although it slightly resembles a creepy ransom note with its jagged cuts and pieces of tape patching it back together, it got to leave the "What the heck was I thinking when I wrote this?" pile. And now it's freaking awesome.

Little victories, people. Celebrate them. Search for those little golden nuggets within your day. And cherish them. The *Michael Kors top in the thick of forlorn and frightening cut-off tees at a ransacked TJMaxx.* So, friend, I pose the question: Is it the **quantity** or the **quality** of the things in your day? I am absolutely not suggesting we all go live in the clouds, blissfully unaware and unconcerned with our "to-do's." It's quite the opposite. I'm challenging you, (and as always, myself) to evaluate that load-bearing list and see what truly needs to be on it. A long overdue phone call? A peaceful walk up to school? A moment of quiet amidst the chaos? Something where you did "*good?*"

And would that be so *bad?*

From the Serenity Prayer

God grant us the serenity to accept the things we cannot change, the courage to change the things we can, and the wisdom to know the difference.

Laugh more. Smile often. And pray over that list. Afterwards, all there is really left to do is The Next Best Thing.

INTERMISSION

I suspend my stories to brighten your world with a short and
sweet snippet from Quinny.

*Lesson learned: people judge. No matter how sweetly you
say "butt cheeks."*

Quinn is my little girl and my baby, so with her older sisters
already at school, she and I did everything together. Her
favorite outing was our weekly trips to the brand-new Hobby
Lobby that began with grabbing fries, soda, and iced coffee at
the closest McDonald's drive thru. And I always rewarded her
ability to let me peruse the aisles, smelling candles and
browsing through extra-large vases I would never actually buy,
with a much-anticipated large bag of Dum Dums from the
check out. *I know, I'm the best mom,* I'll take the award.

She also did most of our grocery shopping with me. While
waiting to check out, Quinn would always attempt to "help"
load things on the belt. This is when her octopus mode would
be in full affect. I *know* I birthed a child with only two arms,
but she grabbed things so quickly I could honestly never keep
up. The minute I would pluck something from her hands and
safely put it down, she had something new but I was now at

the opposite end of the cart and out of luck. This mostly resulted in smashed jars of pickles, apples rolling across the floor and fellow shoppers judging her while she held a bottle of wine. Best Mom Award *taken back*. During one such shopping trip- she decided to, while holding her breakable alcoholic beverage of the day, look sweetly at the stunned shopper behind us and quote the newest movie watched. "Really...a blow dart...in my butt cheeks...."

And there was the *gym instance*. After dropping Q at the childcare, I would bound over to the ellipticals for my well-deserved 20 minutes of peace and Rachel Ray. I would occasionally notice during my sprints and solace that the childcare providers, in their trademark green shirts, would be walking among the exercise equipment, eyes scanning the crowds for the mother of a child obviously terrorizing or who has just pooped. I would then pray they weren't looking for me, completely avoiding eye contact. Sometimes, I think if *I* can't see people, they can't see me. It doesn't always work. So, if I do get caught in a glance, then *sometimes* I point to my earphones and shake my head like I can't hear people when they start talking. But then I remembered I wasn't wearing earphones that day. Darn it. So, I admitted defeat and dramatically trudged off my elliptical, following the older woman back to the room. Next, I heard her say something that makes me giggle to this day.

She looked at me with her sweet wrinkly face, "Ma'am, your daughter just said... (stage note: at this point, she is sternly glaring at me and begins to slowly pronounce every word hereafter) - *Little. Slappy. Make. Daddy. Happy.*"

I almost died.

"Oh, my gosh," I snorted. "*The cloud!* From Trolls? Oh, he's hilarious. She likes to quote movies. It's so cute. And at times, slightly inappropriate...but anyway..."

"Ma'am," the woman interrupted. "You should go now."

Ahem.

"Yes... I probably should...*Quiiiiiinnnnnnn!*"

TURBULENCE

"There are no mistakes, only opportunities." - Tina Fey

DEFINITION-MISTAKE

Websters: "a wrong action or statement proceeding from faulty judgment, inadequate knowledge, or inattention."

Mom definition: being a fun mom and handing out popsicles at 8pm.

I had the privilege of flying out to see my sister while she was vacationing in Maine for a little quick getaway. I was beyond excited for the trip- 3 days of bonding time without the kiddies in such a scenic spot. I even brought my Thanksgiving turkey pants so I could stuff myself with lobster.

But I don't love to fly. Never have.

In order to combat that fear, I surround myself with as many creature comforts as I can to take my mind off this idea of possibly crashing. No, seriously, this is how I think. I wore my comfiest clothes, so I wouldn't be cold on the plane. I packed really good snacks from home, so I wouldn't break the bank at the little newsstand store.

I am such a mom.

BUT I always splurge on an extra-large, extra-fancy coffee drink. Which is not always the best idea to have that much caffeine...on a plane. Just remember that for later. *I think I look very put-together and cool when I'm carrying a coffee.* Like it says, "See, I am so put-together, that I had time to grab a coffee. Not just one from my house in a to-go mug, but from a real, live coffee shop. So, there."

I brought a book to entertain myself; I am ready to independently read, but if someone happens to strike up a conversation with me- I have a bunch of one-liners and interesting facts in my back pocket ready to go. I do consider myself to be the *ultimate* airplane seat buddy.

Fast forward to actually being on the plane: We are all buckled in and I am paying incredible attention to the instructions in the pamphlet in the seat-back in front of me as well as given by the sweet older stewardess. The pilot starts speaking lots of altitude facts and I am attempting to find comfort in his calm and steady voice. It's a nice voice. He probably leads a yoga class when he's not flying. He seems like he knows what he's doing. That's good.

5 minutes into the flight: We are taking off. Oh gosh, I really don't like this part. I wish I had a window seat so I could see. Wait. Maybe I don't want to see. No, I like knowing where I am. No surprises. My stomach feels weird. It's probably better that I look straight ahead. No window. Gosh, Adam is right- I *am* indecisive. We are up in the air now. Phew. We're still alive.

10 minutes into the flight: We are "cruising" now- although the choice of aviation vocabulary has me puzzled. I feel like we are 30, 000 feet up in the sky and might plummet any minute now. I am anything but relaxed. In fact, my heart is beginning to race... nerves... and that extra-large coffee...

15 minutes into the flight: The pilot has given permission to take out toys and such- so I grab my book. Hands are shaking a bit. What did they put in that latte? It's a book on parenting, so I'm pretty sure my seat buddy is going to think I'm a great parent just sprucing up my already great parenting skills.

25 minutes into the flight: I'm super engrossed in my parenting book. The funny thing is- wait for it- it turns out I'm not such a great parent. So, as I am head-deep in my book- studying like I have an exam coming up, foot steadily tapping up and down - my death grip begins to soften. And just as I begin to sit back and relax a bit, I uncurl my sweaty fingers from the spine and covers of the book. At this exact moment, we hit a pocket of air and the plane bumps. Now, out of the corner of my eye, as if dislodged from the slight turbulence, I see the little homemade rainbow-colored bookmark that Quinn drew for me starting to sliiiiip in slow motion from the pages of the book.

Now, in order for you to understand the insane irony of this upcoming situation, you must know something about me. I have *terrible* reflexes and they have honestly only gotten worse over the years. For instance, do you remember the card game "Slap Jack?" When everyone would hit the table every time a Jack showed up in the deck? Well, imagine Monica slapping the table 30 seconds after the Jack was spotted.

Back to the plane ride. As the Quinn-drawn-rainbow bookmark is slooooooowly sliiiiiping out of the pages of my book, the extra-large coffee has hit me 100% and I, ninja-like, LUNGE after the falling memento. I managed to grab it before it fell to the floor, but now awkwardly find my hand in my seat buddy's lap.

Yup. That happened. He quickly glared at me. I returned my hand to its proper place on my side, turned the darkest shade of crimson and mumbled an apology. I pray he heard me. I then quickly threw my head back into my parenting book. Feeling pretty terrible as a parent and now as a human being, I remember that I chose the wrong deodorant this morning. I picked the one that smells good but not the one that works. How much longer is this flight?

30 minutes into the plane ride: The beverage/ snack service is beginning. It has now dawned on me that I need to go to the bathroom. Of course. Darn coffee. I'll wait. I can wait. I'm good at waiting, I have three kids. Why AM I always waiting? My kids should be better at listening. Well, maybe it's that I should be better at parenting. It's probably a bit of both. Kind of depends on the day. Oh, right. That's why I'm reading this book. Because there's a crazy person in my head. Who has to use the bathroom. I feel sorry for my husband.

40 Minutes into the flight: The snack/beverage cart has left, and I now have the world's smallest bag of pretzels and some ginger ale in a plastic shot glass. Why did I get a drink you ask? Because I'm a giant pushover and have trouble saying "no" to people. Even complete strangers. I totally practiced saying "No, thank you..." while I saw the cart coming closer and closer. But when the adorable stewardess asked me if I wanted anything to drink, my hands were clammy and I blurted out, "SURE!" as if we'd be best friends now that I said yes. I have serious issues.

45 Minutes into the flight: I'm back reading my parenting book to distract me when I start to get hungry and my home snacks are not cutting it. Now I think I know how my kids feel. I spot my microscopic bag of pretzels under my magazine on the tray table. Yum. I do love a pretzel. Wait, how do you open this thing? Oh, here's the little cut tab...

*****Spoiler alert: it's about to get awkward again...******

Just as I break into the miniscule pretzel bag (with a newly caffeinated surge), I realize- a little too late-that I am opening it from the bottom. **Hundreds** of tiny salt pieces plus broken pretzels fly all over the place, including all over my seat buddy. How **on earth** did they fit all of that in a tiny little bag? I was contemplating this when I noticed my seat buddy had actually turned his body towards me this time and was glaring. I am going to throw up. I don't like it when people are mad at me.

I KNOW I said "sorry" this time, quite loudly and repeatedly, but for some reason it didn't seem to be helping. It probably did not help that my attempt to clean up my tray table, which was an aggressive and furious sweeping motion, is simply sending more salt and broken pretzels his way, littering his tray table and lap.

Dear Heavens, help me.

∼

Now, I share this ridiculous story with you so that (hopefully) you laugh a little. But also, to share that no matter how you "prep" for your day or plan life- there's always going to be a bit of "**turbulence**," the guaranteed **bumps** of up and down.

It will certainly shift things and you may even ***explode*** and ***fall to pieces*** just like my misconstrued bag of pretzels. But please try to remember one thing if you might be finding it hard to sit back and enjoy the ride: *there's always tomorrow. And decaf coffee.*

IT'S THE LITTLE THINGS

" Don't cry over the past, it's gone. Don't stress about the future, it hasn't arrived. Live in the present and make it beautiful." - Unknown

DEFINITION-BALANCE

Websters: "stability produced by even distribution of weight on each side of the vertical axis."

Mom definition: walking home with three backpacks on one arm, four library books in the other and a Solar System Science project curled on your pointer finger.

Daylight Savings – some people love it. Others, not so much. My kids just don't get it. Still up at 6am- but it's actually now 5am.

I walked upstairs the other morning to see my mom "winding" the dining room grandfather clock. You see, everything either automatically had changed during the night, or we could change it manually to "fall back" to correct the time. But you cannot go backwards in a grandfather clock. You must go forward 11 hours to "go back" one. It took her the better part of 10 minutes to stop on every 15 minutes to wait

& let it chime. Then of course, the hour chimes. She looked quite frustrated.

Interesting that in so many ways, we think that we can control time. We have DVR: the ability to stop, rewind, fast forward "live" TV. We have smart phones that can "slow-mo" a regular video. But meanwhile- life IS happening. We are so caught up in the daily grind, that we gladly, usually without noticing, fly by through the little things.

In the movie *Click*, Adam Sandler's overworked, strung-out, working Dad character is given the chance to control, and ultimately upgrade, his quality (& quantity) of life through an all-powerful remote. He, like us all, doubts its ability at first and then quickly begins to enjoy its fast forwarding, muting, even picture in picture features. He feels like he has been given the chance of a lifetime.

What would you do? Would you pause the good things? Rewind to have a "do over" if you said something you shouldn't have? Or just hit FF through the mundane, sticky situations pounding your daily life until you have gone through it & find the rest and resolve on the other side? If you have never seen the movie, I 100% encourage you to view it- and mostly for its eye-opening conclusion. I love things that make you rethink. And it does.

As I am doing today.

I feel I am incredibly guilty of not always living in the moment. There seems to be so much around that takes my attention away from what really matters. And I'd really like to make a change.

Remember when you only had 24 exposures in your little dinky camera? My hardest test of selection was on our family trips to the zoo. I'd wrestle a little with which animal was worthy of the click, but then - when I was done - I was done. Camera went back into my fashion purse and I went back to reality. Enjoying the moments. But now, we have endless amounts of exposures, re-do's, edits, etc. to get the PERFECT picture. Depicting the PERFECT moment. But was it? It was the 54th attempt with 20 minutes of editing- not exactly worth bragging about.

In college, I would take my camera out with me (I had upgraded from disposable to a Canon) and I'd snap away, still mindful of the inevitability of an empty roll. I certainly did not spend the evening hiding behind a screen. I can happily say I lived it. (It's a perfect sidebar to mention that while I was NOT hidden behind a screen, I was able to see very clearly in front of me. And one fine night, I spotted a perfect Southern gentleman across the room ... and most of you know the ending to that story...)

The next morning, I would walk with my roommates to the school bookstore and send the roll off to be developed. It would take almost a whole week to return. When I finally got them back, I'd be lucky to have gotten 4 or 5 "good shots" out of the 24, sometimes 36 exposures. Mostly, I flipped through 4×6 rectangles of fingers in the way, blurry beyond recognition, heads cut off, and possibly floor shots. And sometimes DOUBLES of these photographic flubs. But, nonetheless, I was thrilled, overjoyed, and grateful to have even ONE photographed "forever" memory from the evening. It was proudly pinned up on my dorm door.

Can I say the same now? I snap away at every park trip, every ice cream cone eating, every bean bag snuggle, and of course- each, every "first" the girls have...because I have deemed them all worthy of documenting and there's nothing technology can do to stand in the way. In fact, it's right there-

encouraging me: to take more, store more, capture more, improve and enhance more. But, certainly, not LIVE more. And live for the NOW. That is something I must decide for myself.

We cannot turn back time. We have no re-do's. We do not have a magical all-powerful remote given to us by Christopher Walken. So, the question is: What will you do with your PRESENT? It is really only here for a fleeting minute. You cannot relive the past-nor should you look too far into the future.

In a past attempt to better "center" myself, I ventured into a yoga class. Sooo many mirrors. I was terrible from the beginning. What did I learn from that night?

1. I am shockingly un-flexible.

2. I am shamefully distractible. (Did I mention all the mirrors?)

3. I did **actually** maintain a fabulous sense of balance ...until I looked around and started comparing myself to others.

I have not been a regular yoga go-er. But I have made some serious connections between the findings from that night and what I've come to learn about myself day-to-day: I am shockingly un-flexible, shamefully distractible, and really do have a great sense of balance...until I look around and start comparing myself to others.

My goal? To ease up, learn to stretch a little with things that initially feel uncomfortable, and to stay focused on what's important. Amidst distraction! And live my life. I think it's possible. I know it is. I'm going to stay positive and strive towards these goals. Won't you join me? ***There's no time like the present.***

FOLLOW YOUR COMPASS, NOT YOUR CLOCK

" Everyone has their own lane, maintain yours...there's less traffic and no speed limit." - Andrea Jung

DEFINITION- WAITING

Websters: *"to remain stationary in readiness or expectation."*

Mom definition: the act of tapping your foot or fingers while your children go back in the house in search of their other shoe. Again.

Love this quote by Andrea Jung. Just love it.

Do you all remember the magazine collages? I used to make them all the time. Slightly obsessed, actually. I would spend hours, days, even weeks creating the perfect collage- **waiting** for just the right word or phrase or picture to complete the ever-so-personalized creation. Why do I bring this up?

Simple.

TIME.

This was a period in my life when there *seemed* to be an abundance of time (teenagers are *so* out of touch), and therefore a lot of **waiting**. I wrote letters, LOTS and LOTS of letters.

To camp friends, the many loves of my life, a sister at college, family... And after I let the envelope slip from my fingers into the deep, dark mailbox on the corner, I **waited**. And **waited** and **waited** some more. That's all you could do!

I **waited** for phone calls. (I shared a line with my parents! Then, eventually, my chatty older sister... #stilllosing.) I **waited** for TV shows to finish... and watched commercials! Sometimes, really awkward ones with my mom. I **waited** for the film I dropped off at the store... and a week later, spent $10 on floor shots! I **waited** for answers to my questions. And then I was told to look up the answer. In the ENCY-CLOPEDIA.

Nowadays, we don't like to wait. I actually would dare to say we don't know how to wait anymore. And if we are actually forced to wait on something, we track it. We track packages on Amazon... Heaven forbid it doesn't arrive in 2 days. We send emails and walk around impatiently then jump across the room when our Hotmail dings, like we've been notified we won the lottery. Every time. We have "read receipts" encoded on our texts- "I know you saw my message... so why are you ignoring me?" *What has happened?*

When I read that earlier quote, I remembered, briefly, what it was like to drive in my own lane- and not get caught up in *when*. The *when* concern is directly connected to the *who*. We are naturally comparative, no doubt about that. And it is even harder not to compare the "who" and "when" in our lives since we are always in the know. And I'm not so sure that's always a good thing.

If I knew of every party, breakup, and new outfit that went on during these "waiting" years, I'm pretty sure I would have been an even hotter mess than I was. As adults, it may not be parties and breakups but, instead, it's pregnancies, new homes, promotions, and so on. It still hurts. Because it's not happening to us.

We tend to think it should all make sense. Like an incredibly easy-to-read road map. Color coded, preferably. In our minds, the fastest way from A to Z is most certainly, a straight line. And some people's lives do follow that course. But not everyone's. Sometimes, Life goes more like C...F......A....K...... Z.....R.....B.....Q... back to C. And that's okay!

It's YOUR journey. No one else's.

Another amazing realization? The only way a compass actually helps you when you're lost is to trust in *true North*. Otherwise, the instrument is essentially useless. What does that mean for you and me? To believe in that true North. Trust that He is guiding you on your perfect path. Even if it seems a bit or even *a lot* out of the way you thought you'd be headed. Find comfort in knowing that the God above who made the world in six days created *you*. And he has some great plans in store.

So, what do you say? The next time the thought, "Hey, why is/isn't this happening to ME?" sneaks into your mind... picture a crowded highway with practically parked cars-everyone going in the same direction. Then, picture a wide open road- with miles and miles of space on both sides. Room to stretch, move, and go your own way. The way you were beautifully and wonderfully designed to be.

364 DAYS OF GRATITUDE

" The struggle ends when the gratitude begins." -Neale Donald Walsch

DEFINITION- GRATEFUL

Websters: *"appreciative of benefits received, affording pleasure or contentment."*

Mom definition: when a friend offers to host the slime making play-date at their house instead.

Speaking of stretching, I love Thanksgiving. It's the time when I scour the house for my stretchiest, comfiest, fill-my-belly-till-it-hurts pants. Please tell me I am not the only one who owns a pair...

Amidst my nightly Hallmark movie watching, there has been more on my *mind* than just my endless grocery list and how I desperately need more flocked trees in my living room. This feast day has stirred up some questions in my *heart*.

Thankful... It's EVERYWHERE...but what does it really mean? And what IS the difference between ***thankful*** and ***grateful***? One definition of ***thankful*** I found was "pleased and relieved." Another was "conscious of the benefit received." While one definition of *grateful* simply stated "contentment." The proper response to an act of giving is to be ***Thankful***. It is why "***thankful*** turkeys" and such cute Pinterest-y activities are preschool appropriate. Even a small child, in their small-minded experience, can be taught to be ***thankful*** for what they ***have***. It makes sense. Although, I seem to have some more work to do with Quinn- her ***thankful*** turkey feathers were as follows: Halloween, candy, Barbies, birthday presents, and Mattie's makeup.

Eek! Clearly, Quinn's mind and heart, in all of her four years, are ***thankful*** for the things that make her happy. No harm in that. She's right where she should be in her understanding. She also puts her shoes on backwards. But how about us adults? Are we still listing things, like Q, that give us comfort, happiness, security, and when services are rendered? Are those the only things that come to mind when we think of being ***thankful***? What happens when we don't feel comfort, happiness, and security?

Let's dive into the meaning of ***gratitude***... I do believe what starts as being **thankful** *can* turn into an **attitude of grati-tude.** Gratitude is a ***way of life***. Seeing the positive in ALL things. ALL THINGS. It's hard. But it can be a game changer. ***Gratitude*** can be unrelated to "what has been done or received." It is almost an explainable joy within the circumstances you have been dealt. Think Cinderella...

Can you see the slight difference? I think I am finally starting to. And I'd like to take Thanksgiving a step further. I'll leave you with a (very personal & not been shared with many) story. I am incredibly ***THANKFUL*** for the opportunity to pursue my dream of being a published picture book writer. There has not been a day gone by that I do not ***THANK the LORD*** for my editor who took a chance on a rising author, as well as my illustrator for bringing light and life to my words.

But to my sadness and disappointment, my much-anticipated book release date was pushed back about a year. That news was hard to swallow. Very hard. I was hanging so much of my self-worth, purpose and joy on that original day. So, when the conversation occurred, my heart sank. There were so many tears and even shaking fists. I have been faithful and fearless. Why was this happening to me?

But I now see that is the wrong attitude to have. I was clinging to the *"what has been given to me" thankfulness.* And when things were going according to my plan, the outpouring of "Thank You, God," was abundant. But when the plan was altered, my *thankfulness* seemed to have disappeared.

This was certainly not an *attitude of gratitude*. Rather, I was throwing a toddler-sized fit. Has God forgotten about my needs? My dreams? Am I being punished? The answer is no. To all of the above. Once I quit my crying about the new date, I resolved that the only way to wake up every day was to pray hard. Then I prayed even harder. I prayed that God would take away my disappointment and replace it with more *gratitude* than ever before about the current circumstances. Circumstances that could not be changed. But *I could be changed.*

I had been so blinded by the book news, that I couldn't see the little blessings and new mercies that filtered in EACH morning. But I knew I wanted to be happy again. Day by day, I began on my knees with a conscious effort to bend those huge daily gripes somehow into little prayers. Full disclosure, I would often yell, sing, or even throw my hands up in an exasperating thanks, usually while doing the third load of laundry. I could be heard miles away, "Oh, Lord! I thank You for this endless pile of clothes worn by my sweet children... I thank You for the dirt, and the spaghetti sauce and the paper they always forget to take out of their pockets... I thank You for *all* of it!" Okay, so it definitely started out slightly sarcastic, but, truthfully, as I belted out each prayer, the truth saturated my words. The devil hates it when you speak the truth. I do have *three* beautiful girls. They *are* incredibly messy, but they are also wild and wonderful. Yes, they are ruining dresses jumping in puddles and ripping their new tights while climbing trees, but they are healthy. And strong. Inside and out. Not all children are so lucky...not all people are so blessed...

Friends, it really did take time, but after a while, I found the kneeling wasn't so hard, and yes, the thanks was still sometimes bellowed...but it really was from the heart. My eyes were opened to the many overlooked joys already existing in my life.

Another opportunity for gratitude was just around the corner. Literally. We bought a house in the neighborhood down the street. And not just any house. *A complete gut job.* Fixer Upper X a million. And THAT, my friends, is what *God knew*. When this house fell into our laps, my heart was full again. Where there was a void of purpose and meaning and fulfillment in my days, He poured project upon project into our lives. Where there was once strife between husband and wife about our future and the 'what if's" and the "why not's" ... there was unity and harmony. And for almost 30 days, we didn't have floors, or sinks, steps or walls, but we had joy. And an abundance of it.

Ahhh. *Gratitude.*

We all have struggles. Some seem monumental. Others- minimal. But we are all engaged in a battle. A battle for our hearts. If we gauge our ***thankfulness*** on simply how life treats us, we are setting ourselves up for a very unstable, insecure way to live out our days. But if we search hard and pursue contentment in the present- no matter what we are going through, we can live out a much more vibrant and meaningful journey. The one we were made for.

Now, try on those ***grateful*** goggles. Mine were a bit out of focus- but with time, my eyes are starting to adjust to what being happy, ***thankful, and grateful*** truly mean. It's a daily struggle, but the reward is great. Won't you join me? I have renewed faith and hope that our future is very bright.

Here's to a ***GRATEFUL Thanks***giving and the 364 days that follow.

MEND OR MOLD...SPRING CLEANING FOR THE SOUL

"Faith is taking the first step, even when you don't see the whole staircase." -MLK Jr.

DEFINITION-CHANGE

Websters: *"to make a shift from one to another, to undergo a modification of..."*

Mom definition: going from yoga pants to clean yoga pants and a real bra.

"A wise woman builds her home, but a foolish woman tears it down with her own hands." - Proverbs 14:1

I've been working on a little something called **"Mend or Mold."** I'll explain more about it in a minute, but first- let me clean my closet.

Why is it so refreshing to purge and throw things away? I think it's because we finally give ourselves permission to let go. Like REALLY let GO. I have always wanted a fun girls night with lots of champagne, preferably an 80's montage, and the sound advice of Samantha, Charlotte, and Miranda to help me discern what should stay and what should go in my wardrobe. But I gave up on that Sex In The City dream a while ago... and have been putting off a real good detox. I suppose I've been convincing myself I'll find the time and place to sport my size 4 sequin dress, with the matching sequin heels. I'm starting to rethink that plan.

So, today I did it. I played my very own 80's montage (quite loudly, I must add) and steadily sipped my extra hot coffee and tossed things to the side. And it felt GOOD to clean things up around here.

Back to **Mend or Mold.** I've always loved alliteration. It helps me remember things. I suppose I could have named this idea *fix it or smash it to pieces with your quick, cold, insensitive jabs,* but that doesn't seem to have the same ring to it. However you phrase it, the premise remains the same: our words are powerful things. Especially the ones that stay in our hearts, poisoning our thoughts, and passing on to the people around us. Usually those closest. Words can lift up or tear down. How, exactly?

mend *verb*

repair (something that is broken or damaged).

synonym- fix, put back together, piece together, patch up, restore

mold *noun*

Molds cause biodegradation of natural materials,

synonym- rust, rot, decay

. . .

Quinn woke me up from a dead sleep the other night and being the good mother I am, I begrudgingly helped her find her teddy, made her warm milk, checked for monsters, turned on her nightlight, etc. As I returned to the room, I frantically - no, more dramatically, fluffed and folded back those sheets as if to make room in our bed for my freshly flown wings straight from Heaven.

Now folks, I share this with you, not to impress you with my incredibly skillful Hollywood- bound acting abilities. Or to even simply highlight what a true saint I am...(hardly!) But rather to add that, believe it or not, I actually practiced some self-control that night. Amidst my frustration that I was NOT sleeping and my husband was sound asleep the whole time, I chose NOT to say something about it. I could've punctuated the scenario with a crass, not really whispering, "You're *welcome*!" Or "Phew, glad *that* is fixed..." Or, shamefully, a comment that has been known to leave my lips, "Are you having *fun* sleeping? " Eek, I know. Not my proudest moments as a human being. But this time I didn't lash out. I chose to MEND. By my lack of utterance.

Do you know what's easy? Being mean. How about being cynical or full of judgment and negativity? Piece of cake. On the other hand- a life with patience, kindness, gentleness and positivity? Now, that's a tough one. I've found it requires a little rolling up of the sleeves and getting dirty while you do some *heart* "clean up."

Working on this house together with my husband has been completely eye-opening. It has shed light on the beautiful bones this house has at its very core and it's been a joy to doctor it to its full potential. I've loved working on projects with Adam- hand in hand- seeing the results of our hard work come to life before my eyes. Give me a paint brush and I'm one happy girl.

But you know what else came to light? House renovations and heart renovations both require serious *tearing* down and patient *building* back up.

My husband would disappear for hours on end- blaring his power tools -shaking and rattling the house and all its foundation. One day, he was down there so long and all I heard was the screeching of his skill saw and the steady pounding of his hammer to the loud beat of classic country- I was 100% **convinced** he was building an ark. He then emerged covered in sawdust from head to toe and sporting a proud smile across his face.

I naturally imagined what AMAZINGNESS I would behold as the girls and I scurried past him, barreling down the basement steps. Yet, when I arrived at the bottom, I saw *no change*. In hindsight, I was only looking on the surface- and that view was pretty sparse. I immediately began questioning the work being done and **added a little comment** unveiling my utter disappointment. This, my friends, is **MOLD.** Spreading slowly and oftentimes in the dark corners of my home and heart. It starts with a single negative word, and before you know, it has taken over my thoughts, actions, and attitude.

A big step toward that renovation is to tackle that foundation. Of our homes and our hearts. As much as it kills me, I just can't go to Homegoods, grab the throw pillows, and decorate studded walls and copper pipes. Work must be done first. The messy, mold – killing, sawdusty, basement kind. And that takes time. And I can't always SEE the progress every day.

In a world of FOMO, and INSTA- everything, our patience and perspective muscles are layered with lethargy. Contrary to what we may think and feel during this pause in our lives, the world has not come to a halt. Things *are* happening. All around. Above and below. Growth is occurring, and often in places we can't see. This is where FAITH comes in. If we practice this little exercise of ***Mend or Mold*** a few moments here and there, we might just wake up one day to find the pipes are working, the walls are up, the mold has disappeared, and wouldn't you know, it's time to snuggle up and make those memories. In the home and in the hearts you've worked so hard to stitch together.

INTERMISSION

Pardon this interruption, as I bring you another quick story from the "Quinn Chronicles."

Lesson learned: things are not always what they seem, especially at the dentist.

At one of her routine dentist visits, Quinn bamboozled me once again. I sat in the tiny room with her, in the adjacent adult seat, thumbing through the most recent HGTV magazine. I occasionally looked up at her to see a cute little face with star shaped sunglasses and precious mouth wide open. The dental assistant was so kind, probing her with tools and little questions she couldn't answer because her precious little mouth was... wide open. I happily dove back into my magazine, reading and snapping screen shots of my next house projects. My DIY daydreaming was suddenly crashed by an ear-piercing scream.

"OUUUUUUCCHHHHH!" I jump up alarmed, magazine flying off my lap, and look over at the chair. The dental assistant was in tears. So was Quinn.

"What just happened?" I asked. I now notice the assistant is cradling her hand in her lap. "She... she bit me."

Oh. My. Gosh.

"Quinny! Why did you bite the nice lady?" I kept questioning her. Nothing but a flood of tears and "I'm soooooo sooorrrrry" came out between her sweet little sobs. I repeatedly apologized to the assistant and incessantly to the dentist- luckily, a family friend. I quickly signed the bill, tucked my tail between my legs, and carried Quinn out to the car. She was still sobbing as I buckled her in tightly. When we stopped at the first intersection, I turned and looked at her, giving it one more try.

"Quinn, honey, why on earth would you bite the kind lady?"

She wiped her nose on her sleeve and said to me, "Because I felt something in my mouth..."

"Yes, Love," I responded. "That's her job. To look in your mouth. And clean it!"

"But it felt weird, like a wooorrrrmmm. I thought there was a worm in my mouth, Mommy," Quinn stated.

"Okay, well, why would you bite a worm?" I inquired.

She looked at me with her big blue eyes, smiling, and said, "*To kill it.*"

Like mother like daughter; My *Wine Spilla* to her **Worm Killa**.

BACK TO SCHOOL: A TIME FOR TESTS

"We are pressed on every side by troubles, but we are not crushed." - 2 Corinthians 4:8

DEFINITION- STRESS

Websters: *"a physical, chemical, or emotional factor that causes bodily or mental tension. "*

Mom definition: Two minutes with Quinn.

"Life has many ways of testing a person's will, either by having nothing happen at all or by having everything happen at once."~ Paulo Coelho.

Back to School! Ah, if life were only like the TV shows and movies. Then *school time* would be a piece of cake. But, alas, life with children is far from how the silver screen portrays it.

Just as we had settled into the groove of Summer with its relaxed schedules, late dinners, and pillow forts under the stars, late August catapults us back into the daily grind, bringing high levels of sweating and a calamity of commitments.

Does anyone stress about school supplies every year? Anyone? Is it just me?? Well, I sure do. I don't just stress, I flat out have a full-on panic attack in Walmart when I can't find the proper size Post-It notes from the list. FULL ON PANIC. Not my best moments. I do manage to calm myself, find my children in the various isles they wander off to, and quietly exit the store. Post-It note-less.

Oh, well.

Then there is packing lunches, buying new last minute clothes (as my oldest child has discovered how easily items can be altered with a pair of scissors!!!!!!!), and of course, the case of the shoes that fit **perfectly** yesterday but somehow *NOT* this morning at 8:15 am. Riddle me that. I have sworn to deep breathe through these moments and not resort to yelling or freaking out. It's a good thing I'm not a betting woman.

But I'm trying. Really, I am. All of this building chaos, however, does bring on some reflection. There are certainly times in our lives when we honestly feel like we are being tested. Put through the ringer. Dragged through mud. Experimented on. Poked, prodded, and pulled in each which way.

Well, folks. You're not crazy. That's exactly what is going on.

I stumbled upon this wonderful set of sermons* dealing with the concept of being tested. They are fascinating and, in summary, explain the four common trials that plague most people:

1. The Pressure Test
2. The People Test
3. The Persistence Test
4. The Priorities Test

Number one poses the question "How will you HANDLE the STRESS you are under?" aka (the dreaded school supplies list). Who/What do you turn to when the waters get rough? Friends? Family? Facebook? Alcohol? There are many opportunities to "run" from our stresses. "If I JUST get to the gym, I know this crazy morning will be behind me." "After my Starbucks triple venti soy skim mocha java non-dairy no-foam extra hot latte, I can take on the world."

But can you? It may bring on even more chances to complain. "I'm just not getting enough SLEEP..." "If only I had an EXTRA set of hands...."

But what IF? Would it ALL go away? I don't know about you, but even after I have been kid-free, massaged, pedicured, and caffeinated, I still blow up at the *slightest* thing once I walk in the door. Why is that? Is it that I am running to the wrong things? Probably and definitely.

Number two poses the question, "What will you do with the DISAPPOINTMENTS in your life that have come from PEOPLE?" Now, this one might *not* make perfect sense at first. It is a question based on the premise that people will inevitably let you down. Not being a negative Nancy, just stating a fact: we are a flawed human race. No one is perfect, so it's bound to happen. If we put all our eggs in someone else's basket, well, we might end up egg-less at some point. (While someone else is enjoying a nice veggie omelet.) I've found that in real life, people don't always play their parts correctly in the crazy, well-rehearsed puppet show in my head. But my problem isn't the people in my life. It's *how* I respond to them when they ultimately don't follow all my crafty prompts and stage directions. The show must go on...

Number three poses the question "Will I KEEP my COMMITMENTS?" This is a test of your character. Are you someone who over-commits? Do you see a clipboard and sign your life away? I sure am. It's a true sickness. We, as a people, tend to spread ourselves a little too thin- thinking quantity not quality in life. In this ever-changing virtual world, it is also easier to back out of things, too. Commit now, MAYBE change my mind later... or not...or maybe I'll go...Sorry, I'm busy. It's sad, but true. Will YOU keep your promises? Or find an excuse as to why you can't...

Number four poses the question "WHO will be FIRST in your life?" This can usually be answered by diving deeper into a subsequent soul-searching couple of thoughts.

· What do you think about the most?

· How do you spend your time?

Imagine your life is a TV documentary and the cameras are always rolling. As they follow you- where are you? What are you doing? Where is your free energy going? Scrolling through our phones? Decompressing in solitude? Reaching out to others?

Life WILL BRING TESTS and trials. Of that, we can be sure. But are we ready? What's in our backpack? An Enya CD and an emergency Snickers bar? Or the little black book full of close friends and verses we can rely on to strengthen us?

"If God brings you to it, He will bring you through it.."

Remember, God isn't asking us to "ace" the course. Or even have most of the answers. Quite the opposite. He knows we're going to stumble with what is put before us. But He also sees your heart, how hard you're trying, and desperately wants to help. All we need to do is bravely raise our hand in the moment and *ask*...

STRONGER

"I can do all things through Christ who strengthens me." - Philippians 4:13

DEFINITION-WARRIOR

Websters: "a person engaged or experienced in warfare."

Mom definition: anyone who throws a birthday party at Chuck E. Cheese.

"No discipline seems pleasant at the time, but painful. Later on, however, it produces a harvest of righteousness and peace for those who have been trained by it." -Hebrews 12:11

How are those New Year's Resolutions going? Why ARE they so hard to keep? There are many theories out there, but I have a few of my own. And my ideas center around the simple, unarguable point that we do not like to struggle. And you have to really wrestle with yourself when starting off and ultimately attaining any kind of goal.

Grass roots of it? It's going to hurt. And it won't be fun. This is the essence of my theory. I'm convinced when things get tough, hard, yucky, ugly, and flat out seemingly impossible- we quit. And by "we," I am using the universal word for ME. But let's take the heat off of me for a quick sec. (Phew, is it getting hot in here?)

And let's dive into my children's weaknesses... Yes. That will make me feel better for a few. I welcomed in the New Year attempting to teach my children about losing & LIVE TV. So many tears and fits over not "Guessing Who" first and why my husband and I are clearly punishing them by subjecting them to all commercials.

I have a lot to learn with my parenting.

As I drive to Philly, my daughter claims she's hungry. I frantically reach into my purse, hoping to find a lint-free lifesaver or something. After a few minutes of unsuccessful searching, I find myself coming up with excuses and kind words to ease her "pain". I finally snap out of it when I realize she's quite capable of packing snacks for the car. And grabbing *both* boots when we leave the house. When did I become such a softie? I mean, I've BEEN one... but I happily tell people I was a way nicer Kindergarten teacher than I am a mom.

But, seriously- why didn't I just tell my kid " You'll survive" – like I was told by my Mom and Dad a million times? And I miraculously DID survive. Grumbling tummies. Bumps and bruises. Team losses. Breakups. Yup. Survived 'em all. My hat is off to my "tough love" upbringing. It sent the message, loud and clear, that truly "what doesn't kill you will make you stronger." And it sure does.

If anyone asked you if you'd like to learn the HARD way or the EASY way, is there any instance where we would actually answer, "The hard way, please?" But we HAVE to. It creates drive, generates perseverance, ignites passion, finds purpose, and propels us into our unique paths. Will we ever know what we are made of, how far we can go or our true limitations if we never fail? Fall? Flop? But first- we must *try*.

And that, my friends, is a valuable lesson I learned one year. I am a heck of a lot tougher than I ever knew. Curl up. In the next chapter, I'd like to share with you a few short stories about my health. But first- a few of my fears: jumping spiders, heights, dentist visits, shots, and basically being in any kind of pain I can't control that doesn't result in bringing a cute baby into the world. Now, let's begin...

WARRIOR NOT WORRIER

" Take one simple step forward in Faith- and then another." - Rosemary Wixom

DEFINITION- MIRACLE

Websters: "an extraordinary event manifesting divine intervention in human affairs."

Mom definition: anytime I get anywhere on time. The word "hallelujah" is usually involved.

Somewhere along my journey, despite my past "survivor" upbringing, I became entirely more of a worrier than a warrior.

My neurotic tendencies as a mom- somehow thinking I can still function solely on cat naps between pick-ups, choruses of Christian music and double shots of espresso- were creating a bit of a storm. The occasional physical therapy sessions provided slight relief but, ultimately, my body seemed to just break down. I called in for a cortisone shot and quickly started panicking. Promised that I was allowed to take anxiety medicine prior to the procedure, I was able to at least walk into the appointment without fainting. Plus, I had the support of the sweetest friend with me to hold my hand.

Fast forward 1.5 hours in the waiting room. I approached the front desk and asked about my anxiety medicine, to which the annoyed woman replied, "You should've taken that this morning before you came. We don't give that here. You are about to be called back." Enter panic. Like hands sweating, can't feel my tongue, heavy legs, room spinning panic. I immediately started to cry, "I can't do this", I kept repeating to myself. "I can't. I just can't."

Well, folks. I had a choice. Get the shot or walk away in pain and schedule something another month out. To me, the choice was clear.

I started to reschedule.

But my dear, sweet friend wouldn't let me. She told me I was strong. And fearless. And could do anything. And reminded me that I wasn't alone. She was here... He was here. So, I trusted her. And Him. And I let both of them hold me. With buckets of more tears, but ZERO meds, I did it.

Phew. That was huge.

But as our minds have it- and I truly believe it's the background work of our earthly Villain- we forget these things. And the next time fear crept up, I was paralyzed again. As if I had completely blocked out how things had gone months before when I was tested, yet trusted and took a huge leap of faith.

In October, I was in pain again. This time, in my abdomen. I wrestled with the pain for a week (hunching over while I walked, still carrying Quinn, and still stuffing Thursday folders...) until, finally, I couldn't take it anymore. The doctor took one look at my face, and checked my abdomen, and immediately sent me to talk to a surgeon. Enter more panic and oceans of tears. I left the surgeon's office with a diagnosis of a large hernia and surgery scheduled for 2 days out. I could barely drive home... I have never had surgery before and the idea of it scared the dickens out of me. And once again, I was faced with more choices. Pain? More damage done to my body if I pushed through? Or tackle my fear...

Amidst my questioning and crying, I tried something new this time. I prayed. HARD. And surrendered. And I decided to trust. And to say I was calm that day is an understatement. Actually, Adam was kinda freaked out by my out-of-character-super-serene demeanor. I just kept smiling at him and saying, "He's got me." And this was without drugs in my system, I promise.

God was unmistakably present through it all.

I am pain-free today. And that taught me a bit more about my ability to face my fears with an army by my side. I felt stronger-ish. Until I had to face my ULTIMATE fear of the.......

DENTIST. Long story short, I had avoided this fear for a shameful length of time, but God said, "It's time," in the form of a cracked tooth. I am now FACE TO FACE with the very scariest of people. (Sorry to all the dentists out there...but, seriously, it's a true fear and I'm not crazy! I googled it... so....)

I had made the decision to be brave and get the work done, but only after I signed my life away agreeing to have "laughing gas" as an aid. They put the mask on. Actually, the poor woman TRIED to put my mask on and once again I panicked. I felt like someone was trying to smother me with a pillow. She told me that the "smothering" feeling was going to be present throughout the whole procedure. It seemed I had another choice. Funny how these things kept coming at me, huh?

At this point, I am hoping you can guess what I chose to do. I plugged my earbuds in, cranked my Christian music ("Fearless" by Jasmine Murray), and gave her the thumbs up. And I survived.

Three different fears. Three moments where I was tested. But with the help of Him who gives me strength and those around me- praying and holding my hand- I survived.

So, back to resolutions. I think too often we ask ourselves, "What happens if I fail?" So we don't follow through or sometimes even try. But we should be asking, "What happens if I never give this a chance?" Take the chance.

I'm only starting to realize God's parenting style is pretty much based on tough love. We will go through the valleys and sometimes in the paralyzing, dark shadows of death... but we should NOT FEAR For HE IS WITH US. His protection and guidance is over our souls- which are in a constant battle. A battle of fear or freedom. A battle of right or wrong. A battle of survivor or surrender. A battle of worrier or warrior.

So, this year, make the resolutions. And try your hardest to keep them. Not because every day you will meet your challenges with bells on. You won't. Resolutions are hard. Life is hard. But keep them because (Phil. 4:13) you are entirely and undisputedly a stronger warrior than you ever knew.

Lesson learned: they're gonna jump.

I spent a good portion of my summers chasing Quinn in my flippy flops, ankles rolling and shins screaming, reaching for her with all my might, praying I could grab that tiny, slippery wrist before a disaster unfolded. However, my scariest moments by the water were not when I *was* chasing her. Rather, when I *wasn't*.

Once, while we were leaving a friendly poolside get-together with conversations ending and amidst the packing up, I heard a sudden and quiet "yip." I looked all around me and saw nothing. Then I realized what I did not see: *Quinn*. I sprinted to the edge of the pool and saw her underwater, eyes wide open. I jumped right in. The rest is kind of a blur, but Adam recalls me scooping her up and throwing her onto the pool pavement. Even the moments directly afterwards aren't all that clear. It's amazing how fear can either paralyze you or send you directly into Momma Bear mode. There's really no middle ground. I had nightmares for weeks playing out the scenario that instead of going into the shallow end and bouncing up long enough to make that sound I thankfully heard- that she fell deep...and silently. The dream would end with my empty arms. The thought still brings me shivers.

As if that particular event wasn't enough to send me to the shrink, she proceeded to hurl herself into waters all summer long. Pools, lakes, oceans. She didn't discriminate. No matter how prepared I was, she managed to continually knock me off my feet. Or out of my new leather boots. Yes, even with a full wardrobe including new stylish footwear, I leapt in and saved her right in the middle of *swim class*. From directly under the nose of a "trained" lifeguard. Nonetheless, the latest and greatest of dear Quinn's aqua adventures does, happily, include a victory. While at the lake this past year, with the assistance of her older cousins, she confidently ascended the tall staircase to the very top of the second story deck, and she *jumped*. Once again, she was fearless. But this time, I was ready. Waiting down in the water, cheering her on, *with arms wide open.*

GOING ON A BEAR HUNT

"Don't let your heart be troubled." - John 14:1

DEFINITION- STUMBLE/TRIP

Websters: "to make an error or blunder. To walk unsteadily or clumsily."

Mom definition: Ahem...I am the definition. Just add beverage.

> *"Going on a Bear Hunt" – American Folk Song*
> *We're goin' on a bear hunt*
> *(We're goin' on a bear hunt)*
> *We're going to catch a big one,*
> *(We're going to catch a big one,)*
> *I'm not scared*
> *(I'm not scared)*
> *What a beautiful day!*
> *(What a beautiful day!)*

Uh-uh!

. . .

"...Can't go **over** it. Can't go **under** it. Gotta go **THROUGH** it." Why is it that, as we tread through life, we seem to do everything in our power to avoid pain & suffering? We certainly do not welcome those growing pains. However, when we have our eyes on the prize, (get that BEAR!), it's so much easier to "take the pain" in stride- understand it, somewhat *appreciate* it. It still hurts, but we accept why it's here. To make us STRONGER.

My favorite group class at the gym is called Triple Threat. My neighbor says, "Well, that just SOUNDS scary!" It is. And I love it. I scream, yell, grunt, and sweat my tail end off- at times, wondering if I'll make it. Why do I put myself through this? Just like any other exercise fanatic, I have my end goal in mind while I think I might pass out and die. So, I press on.

> *Mud!*
> *Thick oozy mud.*
> *We can't go over it,*
> *We can't go under it.*
> *Oh no!*
> *We've got to go through it!*
> *Squelch squerch! Squelch squerch! Squelch squerch!*

Why then do I find it so hard to keep that *same* mentality when LIFE throws its curveballs? I tend to stare blankly and yell, "That's not fair!" like a 2-year-old. Things would certainly be easier if it followed the general rule of checks & balances. For instance – if *I've* been good, *life* should be good. However, that couldn't be farther from the truth. We all know the famous inquisition "Why do bad things happen to good people?" I think of the song "God Bless the Broken Road" by Rascal Flatts and an even older classic "Unanswered Prayers" by Garth Brooks.

Sure, it would be **_easier_** if things went smoothly and according to our plan each and every day. However, where would our motivation be? What would spark our drive? These stumbles and trips can fuel us for the ultimate end prize. Personally, years later, I've come to realise that all those piercing "no's" from editors and agents honestly only made me want to be a writer that much more. I believe there's a beautiful peace that can be found in our lives when you just surrender and TRUST where you're headed, especially when the destination is *nowhere* in sight.

> *Uh-uh!*
> *A forest!*
> *A big dark forest.*
> *We can't go over it.*
> *We can't go under it.*
> *Oh no!*
> *We've got to go through it!*
> *Stumble trip! Stumble trip! Stumble trip!*

Have you ever been part of a team building exercise? You know, the "trust fall" or the "human web"? The point of these activities is to build faith and relationships and encourage you to trust in the somewhat out-of-the-box methods to achieve the end goal- usually *getting to the other side*. How awesome did it feel at the end of those exercises? To look back and see the path taken, with all its twists & turns. It felt good. To trust.

One Sunday morning, I was teaching my girls in "home church" a lesson about Jesus. He was telling his disciples to throw their nets on the other side of the boat after many hours of failed fishing. I love this story. But teaching it to the girls that morning- it took on a whole new meaning. After reading it to them, we watched a cute video, cut out fish from pretty paper, and wove our own little paper bag nets. And before we started gluing them in, I asked the girls why they thought the disciples did exactly what Jesus asked, even when it didn't make sense. "They musta just really trusted Him!" a little voice answered. Yes, my little darlings, they certainly were trusting. And, yes, He knew what was on the other side of that boat. He always knows. We proudly yelled, "I TRUST YOU, JESUS!" while banging the kitchen table and slapping our paper fish into our paper nets. It was fun for them and a powerful lesson on perception and parenting for me.

Why didn't Jesus just blink and "pop" the fish into the nets when he saw the disciples struggling? He easily could have. But where would the opportunity for learning have been? So instead, with a little tough love, He tested them, asking something very out-of-the-box. After scratching their heads a bit, the disciples trusted, obeyed, and great was the reward. "More than their nets could hold..."

> *Uh-uh!*
> *A river!*
> *A deep cold river.*
> *We can't go over it.*
> *We can't go under it.*
> *Oh no!*
> *We've got to go through it!*
> *Splash splosh! Splash splosh! Splash splosh!*

I'm challenging myself to be open to unseen possibilities and to go at life's closed doors with a grateful heart. What can I learn? How can I stretch and lean in? Where am I being asked to throw *my* net? With pain, there is an opportunity to gain. And while we don't always have the answer to why our suffering is present, or why we are only seeing one solitary step at a time, we can still *trust that it's for our own good.*

And so, I attempt to learn yet another lesson from my own offspring. They are fabulous teachers. And singers...

> *We're goin' on a bear hunt*
> *(We're goin' on a bear hunt)*
> *We're going to catch a big one,*
> *(We're going to catch a big one,)*
> *I'm not scared*
> *(I'm not scared)*
> *What a beautiful day!*
> *(What a beautiful day!)*

May you grow strong and courageous through the thick mud, dark forests, and deep rivers in your life. The stumbles and trips are always around the corner, but He promises to be there when we fall. The journey might even produce some endurance and much needed Hope...which are great things to have in this beautiful Bear Hunt we call Life.

SUNFLOWERS AND SURRENDER

"When you are holding on by a thread, make sure it is the hem of His garment." - Toby McKeehan

DEFINITION- INSANITY

Websters: may be defined as "doing the same thing over and over and expecting different results."

Mom definition: waking up on a Monday. After 3 glasses of wine Sunday night.

Stumble. *Stumble.* **TRIP.** Yes, friends- in the powerful words of dear Brittany, "...Oops, I did it again!"

I continue to make the same mistakes and, what's worse, I continue to come out flabbergasted. Are you familiar with the definition of insanity? It is when you do the same thing over and over again *expecting different results*.

So when will I learn?

Take today's little last-minute "grab the end of Summer by the horns" kind of adventure. I ventured out to a special little farm, a place I have wanted to go for years, in the company of our sweet friends. This remote destination is well known for its stunning tulips in the Spring and gorgeous sunflowers in the late Summer. A photographer's dream, truly. Or at least a mom with a fully juiced IPHONE's dream. And a pleasant dream, it started out as...

Car packed with snacks, drinks, DVDs, and the address put into both my IPHONE map and car GPS. Ah, adventure awaits. 30 minutes in: a breezy ride down the parkway, a painless merge onto Route 66, kids happily nodding along to the movie coming through their headsets and some inspirational tunes on the radio. Still living the dream.

10 miles later- Wait. Why is my car GPS telling me to turn around? Google Maps is saying to keep on trekking. Weird. My car is crazy...onward. 10 more miles down the road-car is yelling at me to turn around every chance I get, while Google is saying the exit is coming up. Now the kids are starting to pipe up about popcorn and blankets. This place better be close...

I take the suggested exit, continue down two different dirt roads, and hear the phone say "arrived destination." No farm. No street. I am on the side of the highway, in a ditch, with my flashers on. Cue the kids.

"WHERE ARE WE, MOM??? ARE WE LOST??? THIS RIDE IS SOOOO LONG....." I'll spare you the choice phrases swarming around in my head and the even better ones that eventually slipped out under my breath. I took this time at the intersection of hell and highwater to pause and reset my IPHONE map. Low and behold, it decided to send me 30 minutes back the direction I came from- ultimately synching with the car GPS. *The irony.*

At this point-the movie is long over, the girls have resorted to spitting across the car at each other and some, quite impressively- managed to hit me as well. There is no more popcorn and they have no doubt spilled their capri-suns, between the seats into the tiny space where I will never be able to reach and clean. Everyone is pretty much ***done***. And we have just arrived. Anyone see the massive storm coming?

Well, somehow I didn't.

I knew meltdowns were ***possible***...but I was still convinced I could give them such a good experience that they would forget ALL about their youthful, silly woes and remember why I am the world's best mom.

Some highlights: the three sunflower umbrellas they gave us upon entry became certifiable weapons. The girls fought over the one set of shears I grabbed and ran down the rows of sunflowers yelling, threatening to stab one another, and pitching fits when I asked if I could please cut a flower for myself. They screamed bloody murder every time they saw a bee. The bottles of water that I so proudly remembered to bring got stepped on and/or "accidentally" dumped. They squinted for pictures. They complained about everything.

After 30 minutes, I *surrendered*. We return three baskets more or less in one piece, three sunflower umbrellas- one which won't close anymore now being used to knock over everything fragile next to the cash register, and the mean flower lady asks me to hurry up and pay for my five *dying* sunflowers.

So, there you have it. That was the adventure I kept a secret all morning... told them they would LOVE .... and freak out about... and be so happy. As I do every time. Why do I do this to myself? When did everything get so hard? Is it me? Is it my kids? What is the constant ingredient in this recipe for disaster?

I'm not totally sure. However, I had an epiphany when I got home that day.

It dawned on me during the ride home that my ***expectations were WAY off.*** As they often seem to be. I let perfectionism swoop in and steal the show. Why was I unhappy? Because my kids were acting like kids? Or that I wanted the whole day to play out like a well-rehearsed movie...

If I had leaned into the reality of the situation (that my children were tired, irritable, slightly hungry, thirsty -albeit their own fault on that one- but on a whole- hot messes) before stepping foot on that sunflower field, I think my experience would have been different. Not theirs, necessarily- ***but mine.*** Back to the idea of being tested, this was certainly a "people test." I can't change my kids with a magic wand in these moments, but I can certainly flip through a few of our old classics stacked high on the shelves, pick up a pointer or two and try to adapt ***how I react in the present and future. With a little more grace for myself and a pinch of child- like happiness.***

Repeat after me: **I am doing a great job.** Now, do you *feel* like you are doing a great job? If not, try saying it again- slowly. And please don't meditate on the trips, stumbles, and falls. We are all guilty. Some people are just better at hiding their battle scars. Could we try to make it through the day with a smile hidden somewhere, even a few laughs- if not AT ourselves, then WITH loved ones? Possibly looking at our days through those grateful goggles and not squinting down through the lenses of a critic.

Let us remember that life doesn't have to be perfect. The kids don't. The trips don't. The pictures don't. WE don't. I pray these ideas make their way into your heart and sprinkle Grace and Hope throughout your ***perfectly imperfect*** life.

INTERMISSION

Quinn Chronicle #5

Lesson learned: Don't just fake it till you make it. Own it.

Years ago, it seemed everyone I knew won the lottery for the "White House Easter Egg Roll." For days my feed was inundated with nothing but family photos, everyone all dressed in matching plaids and pastels, historically picturesque backgrounds, and joyous moments. I was super jealous. And then, I had my chance. We were offered tickets and the planning of our epic frame-worthy photos began. However, Mother Nature had the last laugh. A morning cold front brought fog and spitting rain, frizzing all the straightened hair and causing us to cover our cute correlating outfits with unattractive bulky coats. When we arrived on the White House property extra early- which is beyond ironic because I'm always late- and saw nothing was even ready, the girls simply dogpiled and screamed bloody murder. We chased down a freakishly large rabbit for an awkward family photo and then took our place in line for the epic "Roll." I petitioned Adam to hurry up and get his phone ready to film, but quickly realized the girls were already halfway done. Autumn finished first, followed by Mattie, but my view of Quinn was completely blocked. I forced a smile, sad to have missed seeing them *all*.

When we got home that night and flopped on the couch reminiscing the tales of the day, Adam pulled out his phone and with his trademark sneaky smile proceeded to show me the videos he captured. And there it was: Quinn in all her egg rolling glory. While her sisters had raced ahead, she just stood there at the starting line looking completely puzzled. At first swing, she lifted the egg, sending it flying *sideways* across the marked lawn. A volunteer quickly retrieved it and she got right back to it. She swung and swung and swung...ten more times. Determination oozing and her cute little tongue sticking out with every swing. *Never* to make contact with the egg again. And, afterwards, she strutted across that White House lawn *like a boss,* threw her arms up in the air, and *celebrated anyway*.

On my tough days, I brew super strong coffee and sit on my back porch hammock, watching this video over and over again. It brings me *serious joy* and almost seems to make everything else fade away. Until the next **momergency**.

INTO THE UNKNOWN

"Weeping may last through the night, but Joy comes in the morning." -Psalm 30:5

DEFINITION- COMFORTABLE

Websters: "enjoying contentment and security, free from vexation or doubt."

Mom definition: wearing my husband's sweatpants and watching hours of uninterrupted Hallmark. Preferably with chocolate nearby.

Yesterday started off with the sun shining and birds chirping as I sipped my coffee on the porch while reading a daily devotional. My hair was even brushed. But the day quickly spiraled downward and even ended in tears. Some days, it really does feel like you are on top of the world and then, moments later, you're lying flat on your face.

I'm a very passionate person and, in fact, in our pre-marriage counseling, it was discovered that my husband is subliminally and sublimely attracted to me because of my ZEST for life. And *I* for *his* manly, rock solid attitude. Let's go with that. But, seriously, I approach life pretty positively. That doesn't mean I'm not going to get tripped up on things. Quite the opposite. It means that *when I do TRIP, TRIP, STUMBLE*, I risk falling pretty hard. Those mountain tops are really high...

In church I learned about a term incredibly relevant to my chaotic life - "commitment move". It's actually a rock-climbing term. This refers to the inevitable situation climbers find themselves in when they must leave the security of their current sure grip and reach for another.

Now, in life we tend to gravitate toward SURE and COMFORT. Can you blame anyone? You are talking to a woman who lives in pjs and wool socks and loves pillows, checklists and routines. Being comfortable and sure feel really good albeit boring, slightly mundane and, to go back to rock climbing, completely STUCK. Think about it. If one is hanging on the side of a cliff and *never makes a move*, one remains on the side of a cliff. And do you know when it's impossible to make that move? When your one hand is barely clinging to the Truth- your foundation in Faith- and your other hand is **full**. Of laundry, dishes, backpacks, shopping bags, lists, commitments, and questions. How can you reach with everything so tightly wound? Truth is- you can't. And this is where the villain of our story makes *his* best move *yet*.

The devil wants **nothing more** than for you to stay. He desires you to remain, **cliff hanging**, stranded between known and unknown. It is at this point in the game when he increases your insecurity while decreasing your courage. He is the Father of Lies- whispering whatever he can to fuel your confusion, worry, wonder, and doubt. When you look back, you only see struggles and failure. When you look forward, you experience paralyzing fear. You feel completely ensnared. And if he sees you leaning forward, boldly reaching for that next best thing, he'll start to play *dirty*. He'll flood your life and you will feel like you are drowning. Marriage- straining.

Children- disobedient. Home- chaos. Friends- silent. He will make you believe you are utterly alone. He will pry you away from your faithful foundation, one finger at a time. He will poke at your patience, steal your peace, jostle your joy, loosen your love, and finally, he will attempt to snatch away every ounce of your Hope. He waits for you to fear, fail, and eventually, too weak to hold on any longer, **fall.** And he thinks he has won.

And he does win *some* battles. He won yesterday. He won it *good.* I was defeated. I yelled at my kids constantly. I felt lucky to get two consecutive sentences written before an interruption-usually the sound of perpetual arguing and neediness. And at one moment, when my favorite framed mirror was knocked off the wall and shattered into many pieces, I simply exploded into a mess of tears. My head hurt, my neck hurt, my heart hurt. So I blamed my husband, molding the situation with complaints and negativity, my grip slipping. And as I tried to sleep, I dreamed of nothing but a never-ending *fall*.

But, dear friends, I woke up this morning, reached up, and remembered my story is far from over. Repeat after me- the devil may have won that battle, but he will NEVER win the war. Say it again with me, louder. Shout it. Own it. And why? Because the war has *already been won.* By a Savior. He restores my patience, peace, joy, love, and Hope each morning. And with this fresh dose of Hope in my heart and in my hands, the girls and I began gluing the broken pieces of my precious mirror together into something new.

As you bravely get ready to make *your* next "commitment move," I pray you overcome the heavy pull dragging you backwards to the sureness and security of only what is known and understood. I pray you turn away from the lies whispered to you in the quiet darkness that say "you can't." I hope you feel encouraged by your renewed strength, confident to stretch- reaching higher and trusting in the unknown. *Your unknown, **but not His.** Cling to His sure comfort. It's the only hand that will never let you down.*

INTERMISSION

This break is brought to you by the next installment of the "Quinn Chronicles."

Lesson learned: like a moth to a flame...big and bouncy wins every time.

I lost Quinn. There, I said it. And it was the longest and most gut-wrenching twenty-six minutes of my life. Not the "come out, come out, wherever you are hiding in the clothes rack" kind. No. The "frantically roaming store to store at a mall, heart beating out of my chest, showing pictures on my phone" kind of lost. The stuff they make movies about. Or Dateline specials. My mind raced from thought to thought, never arriving at any reasonable conclusion or decision. I was legitimately walking in circles. The only thing I did know was that I left a changing room *with her*. And then she was *gone*.

I remember telling my friend who was with me. Her panicked look said enough. But her calming hug said more. Zero judgement. Just another momma bear now on the hunt. She told me she would take the bigger girls and that we should split up. I went to the coffee store, ice cream store, jewelry store...everywhere I could run to. With legs like jello. Most people waved me off with a quick, "Sorry, I haven't seen her." I felt the weight of their eyes judging me as they each responded to my shaking voice.

"I can't do this," I whispered. As I flipped through the pictures on my phone for a kind stranger, the hot tears flooding down my face would not stop.

I melted into the closest booth at the food court. I didn't know what was hurting more. My head or my heart. "I am an awful, awful, mother", I kept repeating to myself, over and over again. I have thought these exact words many times before but never believed them so clearly. The syllables made their way from my mind to my lips, and I started to whisper between my sobs.

It was only when Autumn zoomed back to gawk at a massive bounce house directly down the hall from the restroom, face glued to the wall of windows, did I finally hear the relieving words, "I found her!" I stumbled down the hall, barely seeing through my tears. When I felt Quinn's little body press up against me, new levels of hormones came rushing in. And I have *never, ever* ugly cried like that. Well, *in public. So,* the very next day, I bought a kid leash. And have never looked down on another mother who uses one since. In fact, that day, I joined a team of proud parents everywhere. Those who are working really hard not to *lose their kids* and working even harder not to *lose their minds*.

A LIFE FULL OF MORE

"He came so we may have Life and have it to the Full." - John 10:10

DEFINITION-DEDICATION

Websters: *"self-sacrificing devotion and loyalty."*

Mom definition: listening to nonstop princess music instead of Top 40 on three-hour-long car rides.

Have you ever been a part of a surprise? It's such an interesting setting to watch play out- whether you are the decoy, the distraction, the planner, or the recipient. There's always *more* than meets the eye. The "behind the scenes curtain" is being held up with loads of faith, trust, and hope that it will *all come together in the end*.

While my husband and I were dating, we had a standing Wednesday night date. Come heck or high water, we made this date happen. It was a clear, dedicated, and committed expression of young love. ***A promise kept,*** week after week. However, one Wednesday afternoon on my ride home from teaching, I received a phone call from Adam, breaking our date. I distinctly recall the slow heat coming over me, resulting in flat-out furious. Where was his commitment and dedication? Didn't he understand the incredible weight riding on that weekly date? It basically held us together in those years we lived far apart. Like relationship tape. He ripped quickly, but the pain was still felt deep in my heart. We had been off-balance for months. The dreaded stage where one part of the team wants to get married while the other isn't quite ready. It was larger than an elephant in every room, in every conversation, and it was molding our presence together. I was constantly overwhelmed with feelings of not being good enough and wondered about our next steps.

So, as you can imagine, I expressed my continued disappointment and frustration on that phone call. For over an hour. He was very quiet, just taking the punches. I think that was making it worse. Why wasn't he fighting back? Although a time or two, I remember him gently asking me to please *trust him*. It's really only fair that at this junction I mention that the last time I heard a repeated "trust me" from Adam, he had asked me for my ring size and blindfolded me for an entire car ride that ended at a bowling alley. Where I was quickly gifted with a sparkling, personalized bowling ball.

Well, friends, it seemed the love of my life had planned another surprise and, this time, the motive was unquestionable. Approximately one month later-following a moment of true peaceful surrender on my end- clarity, dedication, and commitment came. In the form of a beautiful, sparkling diamond ring. That sweet boy had canceled our date weeks before to drive up to Philadelphia and have dinner with my parents. And, ultimately, ask for my hand in marriage. He may have broken our date that night, but, in the end, he strengthened *his promise*.

. . .

Now, on to Easter Monday. Even though we were restricted to staying home for spring break, I took the girls on a bit of a journey- *behind the scenes* of Holy Week.

We walked next to Jesus, celebrating and waving Palms.

We turned tables with Him, angry, in the Temple.

We watched as Judas betrayed Him - choosing money over friendship.

We were humbled as He washed the dirt and day off *our* feet.

We broke bread and drank wine with Him.

He told us He would be leaving soon. That it was *all part of a plan*.

We prayed with Him in the Garden.

We fell asleep and woke to soldiers taking Him away.

And He said nothing to escape it.

He only told us to *trust* Him.

He was mocked, scourged, beaten, and accused.

He stayed silent.

Then He was nailed.

And He breathed His last breath.

Why?

For them. For *us*.

The girls and I sank deep into the honest thoughts and actions of those disciples. His closest friends. How forlorn they must have been. How confused and utterly hopeless they must have felt. Only seeing death, they didn't know there was *more to come.* But **we do**. We have *Hope*. We know that the "Good" on Good Friday was there indeed, amidst the pain and suffering. What happened 3 days later brought more life and light into this world than death and darkness could EVER try to hide. Just at the very moment when all seemed lost and broken, the Hero of our story rose up, ringing the victory bell. And that same victory and HOPE is still with us today.

Speaking from someone who dreads taking down the decorations and drowning in the post-holiday blahs, I truly believe it *can be different*. The message of Easter did not get lost among my perfectly positioned pastels and pastries. Those things weren't around this time. What was **a clear, dedicated, committed act of love.** And I felt it deeper in my heart than in any past Easter. (And I'm a Preacher Kid- so I've had my fair share of triumphant trumpets, layers of lilies, as well as epic egg hunts.)

Maybe it was because my heart was desperate for a sign: a positive *promise* to overthrow the negative nightly news. Or maybe I have finally learned that brick and mortar buildings, dozens of decorations, and matching outfits do not an Easter make. It isn't something that can be bought, taken down, and put back up every year. It's **more. It's a promise kept.** A **sustaining feeling** that can brighten the darkest of days, the most somber of circumstances. **If** we let it.

So, after you toss out the colored eggs, package up the bunnies, and box up the cute checkered baskets and banners-resist the temptation to feel down. You won't need them where you're headed. Today can be the FIRST day of a new season, a year, a life ... *full of Hope*.

~

I'm no Dr. Seuss, but I gave it a whirl...

What does our future hold?

What will this all bring?

I cannot say exactly.

But I am certain of one thing:

Hope *already won.*

So, push **Dark** *out the door.*

Cling to His Love,

And a Life full of More.

'TIS THE SEASON FOR CHAOS AND JOY

" Peace I leave with you, my peace I give to you. Not as the world gives, do I give to you. Let not your heart be troubled, neither let them be afraid." - John 14:27

DEFINITION- JOY

Websters: *"a state of happiness, felicity or bliss."*

Mom definition: the moment when my children are finally asleep in their beds.

My favorite season is upon us. Christmas. So much Joy. And, in this time in my life, a little chaos. Let's start by deep breathing and thinking of some peaceful images to ease our minds... swinging in a hammock near the seaside, a quiet moment on a dock with a steamy cup of coffee and watching the sunrise, or cuddling on a couch near a roaring fire and watching your favorite movie.

Did you find your Zen place? I have one more image for you...a mother bird hovering over her nest perched atop a tree branch that is over-stretching a raging waterfall.

Ahhh- wait. What? How is this an image of Peace? I'll get to that. But, first, a question for you. **What is your thing?** You know, the *thing* that brings you the most Zen, peace, joy, and happiness? Do you have it in your mind? Hold onto it while I tell you mine: order and tidiness. It brings on a beautiful euphoria that calms me and pleases my senses. My Kindergarten classroom had a million bins with pretty labels. But that was then- and this is now. I have a family with three crazy kids! The expectation to achieve and maintain order is like a dog chasing its tail. It's honestly never going to happen. If an orderly kitchen brings me peace, then what on earth am I going to do when inevitably one of my children comes in, soaking wet and covered in dirt, releasing little spots of gunk everywhere like a shaking dog? It breaks me. And the cycle starts all over again: work hard, freak out, grumble, clean, repeat. My story's villain is back at work.

When does this insanely flawed sense of peacefulness make its ultimate fail? Anytime there are expectations, tests, cliffs, and long windy roads up ahead. As the December month dawned, it seemed as if everything I tried to create, experience, and or do had a Christmas *curse* on it.

My children all had epic freak-outs on the top of a mountain after an almost two-hour journey to capture the perfect Christmas tree. I proceeded to state the importance of this day I always try to recreate from my childhood and with exasperated syllables grumbled, "You...need... to... get... up... off... the... ground... and... smile..." After insane threats and lots of judging from strangers, we managed to cut the tree down, salvaging smiles for a forced family picture. If you only saw the moments before and after. It was a long ride home.

Then there was the tree trimming that I pretty much did all by myself with multiple light strands powering out through the next couple days, cookie baking where I almost poisoned everyone, and the neighborhood present-delivery that ended with scrapes and cuts. Not good. Not good at all. I continued to approach each situation from my crazy, overzealous, "Hallmark" heart, and each time, life continued to *fall short* of the movie version. To me. But never to my kids. They don't have the same perspective to warp an entire experience into a complete and utter disaster. They can't even remember what they had for lunch. They just have kid brains. And *huge hearts*. When you hear about "experiencing Christmas through the eyes of a child", I think it's a pretty smart idea. Kids get excited, don't overthink, or even think at all sometimes. They drink it in... perfect examples of joyfully living in the moment.

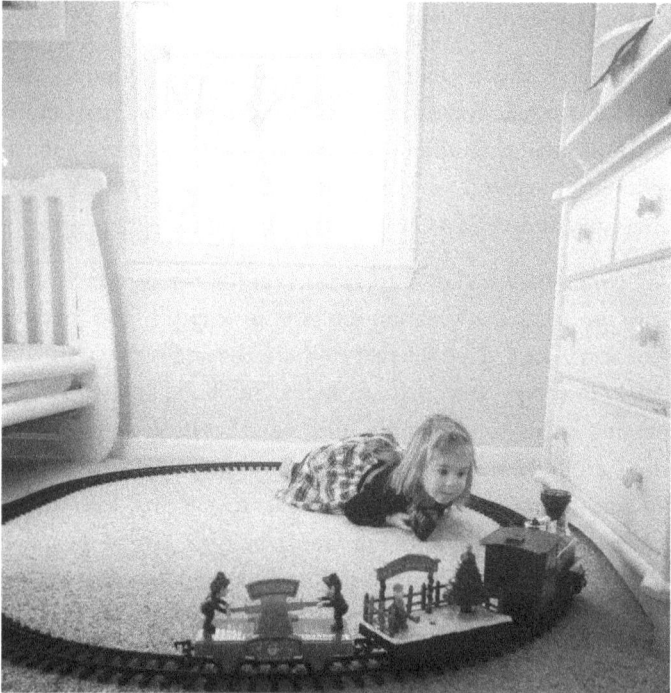

Life is usually messy and loud and unorganized- which is when the joy thief tends to claw at the back door. Will over-analyzing and over-evaluating everything prepare you for the unexpected? Or leave you exhausted for the next round of your wonderfully imperfect life?

What would happen if you and I looked up and asked for a new sense of peace? Not the organized kitchen kind, but fully immersed in life's chaos *and yet feeling peaceful*? Is it even possible? Well, friends, I gave it a try.

Funny thing about praying for peace and patience, God might just throw you some curveballs to get you swinging...

∾

I loaded up the girls and headed to the Gaylord Hotel outside DC. Every year, we visit Santa, ride the train, search for Gingy, the giant gingerbread man, and do all things Christmas. It is certainly a memorable day and each year brings *new challenges*. This year, there was so much running, excitable yelling, jumping in front of strangers, insane elevator button pushing, and awkward pointing that I had many chances to lose my cool. *Almost*, when my children were consistently photobombing other family pictures. I thought the glares from the other mothers would send me crying. But they didn't. *And almost*, when all three girls tackled each other in the middle of the reception area, hurling their snow boots and knocking over magazine-worthy trees.

There were many many tears.

But, *not mine*.

In moments when I would've normally lost my mind, I stayed surprisingly calm. I cleaned up my puddle of children from the floor, gathered their lost articles, and we went on our way. I waited for the freak out in the car on the way home. Still nothing. Where was this calmness coming from? This was weird. Ah, I just remembered I swapped out my normal morning coffee for herbal tea this week. Yes, that must be why. No, I just treated myself to a Starbucks on the way here. So that wasn't it. Could it be because I switched deodorants? I've come to believe that motion- sense stuff is a sham. True- I smelled quite nice, but still, it couldn't just be that...

And then, I remembered what I prayed for. A sense of peace and joy – among all things. Not a PEACE-FUL Christmas, but rather a child-like wonder and happiness in our chaos. And there it was.

~

Back to the image.

What does this bird have to do with you and I? This creature has a home atop a birch branch that is outstretched over a *raging* waterfall. Should it worry? Fret? Lose sleep? Lose Hope? Move to a safer habitat? Or will troubles follow no matter where she is resting? The amazing thing is this bird *is* peaceful. Right there, submerged in thundering, frightening circumstances.

And that is my grown-up Christmas wish for you, friends. That you experience a renewed, deep PEACE (*"PEACE I leave with you; my own peace I now give you. Not as the world gives, do I give to you." John 14:27)* Not the temporary calm that comes from an hour at the spa, a super clean and organized kitchen, or even achieving that perfect postable picture moment. Think about how easily those things can be taken or ruined. I wish for you the joy and calm that comes only from HIM and letting Him hold you. ***Amidst all the storms of life.***

Isaiah 9:6 For to us a child is born, to us a son is given; and the government shall be upon his shoulder, and his name shall be called Wonderful Counselor, Mighty God, Everlasting Father, ***Prince of Peace****.*

INTERMISSION

Another brief peek into life according to Quinn...

Lesson Learned: Keep the Champagne on Ice

When Quinn was finally old enough to attend the preschool's Vacation Bible School with her sisters, Adam and I figured we'd get our first alone time in forever. For 4 straight nights. Can you imagine? I'm always the last to get my paperwork in, but- for that- I was filling things out on my phone and in my bed, the minute I got the email. We dropped them off, (actually more like *pushed them* in the preschool doors,) and ran back to the car like teenagers sprinting from stern parents. Then Adam and I went back to the house and did absolutely nothing. But we did it kidless and, most importantly, Quinless.

Two and half hours later, we got back in the car, windows down, music blaring. Life was good. *However,* when we arrived that first night and split up to collect our girls, my kidless escapades came to a halt. I turned the corner to the classroom and saw all the other kiddies carrying their treasures, smiling ear to ear, and hugging their adults. I scoured the tiny table outside the room for Quinn's items, but saw no treasures with her little name on it. As I moved through the sea of parents and approached the teacher, she just pointed her finger. The poor woman looked like she had been through a war. I spied sweet, innocent Quinn sitting on the floor, pouting and playing with her chubby little fingers. Apparently, she declined to eat the snacks, repeatedly roughhoused with the other kids, then punched her best friend. Oh, and she *kicked* the teacher.

When Adam arrived with our other two girls in tow, he couldn't help but laugh at her shenanigans. I, on the other hand, almost died of embarrassment. So, however compassionately they prayed for my little angel's behavior to drastically take a turn, their fervent prayers were not answered. Quinn will be Quinn. So, by the third night— however you spin it- she was pretty much uninvited to return.

To a church camp. And FYI- her teacher quit.

FAITH LIKE A CHILD

"For I know the plans I have for you, declares the Lord. Plans to prosper you and not harm you. Plans to give you a future and a hope."- Jeremiah 29:11

DEFINITION- REST

Websters: "freedom from activity or labor."

Mom definition: beach vacations. 10 years ago.

My middle child, Mattie, is a real actress. Not a day goes by without some kind of Broadway production. She is so much fun. One evening, I was watching her experiment with a new magic kit. It was full of little trinkets, sparking wonder and curiosity for her, and-in theory- engaging her future audience. At one point during the first of such shows, I could clearly tell she was struggling. The ball was not exactly disappearing. To her credit- she just kept trying and trying, all the while wearing her best smile and convincing me something *amazing* was about to happen.

Nothing amazing happened. And when I asked her, "Mattie, did you read the directions that came with the kit?" she quickly and confidently responded, "No." Bless her heart. There was another five more minutes of struggling, and throughout that time, I got to see the ins and outs of the actual trick. So, when it came time for the BIG reveal, I smiled back at her and allowed myself to fall fully into her magical debut. I marveled at how she, too, was falling fully, believing 100% that she had unleashed powers beyond imagination. I love my children. They really do encompass an innocence when it comes to **believing**. And I was re-reminded of this while watching Mattie and her simple yet constant "One, two, threeee!!!!!" Nothing like a good old fashioned magic trick to showcase how easy it ***used to be*** and ***should be*** to "believe without seeing."

Fun fact: I haven't slept since the 80's. And as a result, I never have been nor will ever be that mom who looks amazing at morning drop off. I wish I could say I rock a baseball cap and huge sunglasses like the celebrities when they go "au-natural" and are trying to be fashionably incognito. But when *I* try that, I'm pretty sure the girls' school thinks there's a homeless guy staying with us who is always carrying a to-go mug of spilled coffee. But back to my lack of rest.

I have only recently made a huge mind-blowing connection that I can't fall asleep while being a control freak. It may sound obvious to you, but I had always associated my insomnia with my creative juices flowing when it was *finally* quiet. But, through the second go around of a lesson at my weekly Bible study, my mind and heart were opened to what is truly missing in my life. And it's not just a good set of ZZZ's.

Faith.

Trust.

Peace.

It turns out a life lacking in such things leads to surefire unrest. The bright side? My best defense might be as easy as 1, 2, 3.

One- It's DONE! This, my friends, is referring directly to my inability to let go of the *past*. I hash out the parts of my day- things I've done and not done, said and not said. I'm actually exhausted just typing this out. But it's true. 100%. I feel like I'm watching the unedited movie version of my past from up in the cheap seats while throwing popcorn at the tiny screen. What can I change at one o'clock in the morning? If I would simply have more PEACE in my day- the messes and mistakes, highs and lows-my head might hit the pillow with a deeper sense of "It is Good." Not perfect, but how it *should* be.

When interviewing my sister Rachel on her 3rd anniversary of sobriety, she gave me advice I keep very close to my heart. I am humbled by the beautiful and hopeful outlook she has on life, saying goodbye to the old and choosing the new every day.

"It's nice that you work through The Steps, and you let go of the guilt and shame. You let it go. And as you let it go, doing the steps, you are free-er and free-er and happier and happier. You just let the past be the past. And accept that things were done, and it's okay. It is okay... you made mistakes, but that was another you. This is a different you, and this is the real you, and this is a better you. It's all not consuming you. It's amazing- you just let it go. Like a confession to a priest... you just let everything go."

My sister is now holding onto something she never quite believed in before. Although it's not an illusion or a magic trick, it does unleash powers beyond her imagination. Powers to overcome. She has found the healing, saving grace from a loving God. And this same amazing grace fills her and washes away the footprints of her past. Every day.

Two-IT'S NEW! I'll never forget the time I took Mattie to get her first pair of glasses. Her big brown eyes lit up behind the little lenses when she put them on. I sat there and wondered what she was seeing for the very first time. When we got in the car and started on home, I heard her begin to mumble in the backseat. I listened for most of the car ride, unable to figure out what exactly she was saying. At the next stoplight, I turned around to see her face pressed firmly up against the window, clouded with her own breath, while she recited what sounded to be number after number. I quickly glanced around to see what she was looking at and suddenly I noticed it, too. House numbers. Until that very car ride home, my sweet little Mattie had never seen the pretty little numbers adorning everyone's roofs, doors, and mailboxes. Her world just got bigger, brighter, and more beautiful in those very moments. What a gift.

I've come to realize we've been given a unique gift each morning- a brand NEW day. A chance to see things and do things differently. Opportunities waiting, like the unwritten pages in a book. Or even, like a whole new world just outside your window. However, may I be mindful of how I need to pick up the pen and clipboard a little less and look up a whole lot more. What is going on around me at this very moment? What can I see? It's truly a *present*. Have I opened it? Enjoyed it? Sometimes the next best thing is just *faithfully* being there, noticing things. Your family doesn't want the whole world. They just want *yours*. Messy hair, baseball cap, sunglasses, spilled coffee, and all.

Three- You're FREE! In case you haven't guessed it- this one relates to the *future*. In hindsight and much agonizing reflection, I have learned that THIS is the part I struggle with most. I desperately want to know what's coming. I want to be prepared and even a step ahead of the next move. I'd prefer the guarantee of fewer worries. Fewer failures. For my girls, my husband, my friends, and for me. But I also want to live peacefully on the edge of that raging waterfall, trusting.

If you're not going to take my word for it- that having all the answers and seeing things written in newspapers 10 years ahead does not, in fact, bring peace, happiness and joy- then take it from Doc Brown and Marty McFly. They're time traveling experts *from the future*. I'm convinced- thanks to these fine gentlemen who dared to dream and create the fluxcapacitor- that if I had all the answers, there would not be an increase in peace and joy. Instead, it would leave me unbalanced and weighed down with more questions, more wonders, and striving for more control. I must try to fix my eyes upwards, steady on that horizon, even amidst the storms. I don't always need to know what's coming. But I can seek to open my heart a little more and **Trust** that it's all part of an incredibly well thought-out plan. A plan full of Hope.

When I have peace in my past, live faithfully in the now, and hand up my future, I am **Free.** Free from fear. Free from perfection. Free from knowing it all. Free from holding it all. Finally, I'm Free to *rest.*

So, my sweet friend, could it, should it, be that easy? Life isn't exactly like a child's beginner magic set. But, as I tuck my children into bed at night and watch them cozy and peaceful, not a worry in the world, happy with the day behind them and excited for what's up ahead, is there any harm in having a little more *faith* and *believing like a child*?

WHEN GOD SENDS A SLEIGH

"I lift up my eyes to the mountains—where does my help come from? My help comes from the Lord, the Maker of heaven and earth." - Psalm 121:1-2

DEFINITION: HELP

Websters: *"make it easier for (someone) to do something by offering one's services or resources."*

My definition: my Heavenly Father's strong and steady hand. Holding me, carrying me, guiding me, restoring me.

I am carrying 8 heaping bags of groceries through the nearby woods. *The bags are breaking and my fingers are completely numb.*

I suppose I should back up a bit.

Many years ago, when I lived in Maryland in a house full of fabulously fun teachers, I often walked to the nearby mall and grocery stores whenever I needed anything. It was great exercise and I loved being outside. However, time and time again, I would get lost in the land of shopping- grabbing Costco-sized items and making myself proud with all the steals and deals. It was only at the very moment when I pushed my cart outside that I ultimately realized my sole transportation home was my pair of Uggs.

Now, you may be saying to yourself, there's absolutely NO WAY I did this more than once. Sadly, I must admit such ignorance. And back to my story.

I mustered up the hand strength and grabbed my 8 bags of groceries and started off through the woods. I sometimes stopped a time or two, but stubbornly decided that if I kept going- ignoring my blue fingers, breaking bags, and screaming shoulders- I could make it. And I always did make it home, proudly avoiding anyone seeing me struggle in the streets. Until the one day when I was caught.

I had ignored Adam's texts dinging in my pocket – OBVI-OUSLY with no way of reaching my phone. He knew I was out shopping and, being a smart lad, after seeing my car in the driveway, *figured* I had tried something like walking home with 20 lbs. of groceries. Can you see why we are married? I'll never forget when I realized he was trailing me. It was the sound of a snicker sneaking through the truck window, accompanied by his notoriously loud but adorable karaoke-style country music singing. I tried hard to conceal my smile.

But here's the real kicker. As relieved as I was to see (and hear)Adam, I didn't let him help. I gave some excuse about how my fingers would fall off if he even tried to un-bag them with his manly ways, somehow convincing him that I could make it the 2 blocks home. And he reluctantly agreed. But not without trailing me... with a little more snickering and a lot more sweet serenading. When we got to the house, I was so mad at myself with the worst pins and needles in my aching hands, that I hurled some *mold* into the situation- yelling at him for something about *never being there for me*.

I feel I should give you the time now to give me some kind of a polite shove. I needed it. I was so bent on being indepen-dent and relying *on my own strength* that it blinded my judgement and understanding. And didn't allow the help to actually help. It amazes me sometimes that I could be that dense. So very, very long ago.

Oh, wait. I'm still doing it. I am still putting 20 lbs. of groceries in my hands. Not literally any more- THANK HEAVENS I'VE LEARNED ONE THING- but figuratively. I still get wrapped up and weighed down, striving for some award if my house is super clean, or my laundry is all caught up, if I chaperone a field trip, or buy all my kid's favorite foods for lunch and dinner. But the Truth is I'm not being given any earthly award or bonus points for those things. In fact, the real problem begins if I put all my Hope, Faith, and Joy *IN* those things. Each of them can be snatched away at a moment's notice. The house gets trashed in 10 minutes after the kids get home from school. The laundry quickly doubles and overflows. I can't fulfill my commitment at school anymore for one reason or another. And suddenly, the girls have changed their minds on what flavor mac' n' cheese they like, so now I have a dozen boxes they won't touch. The bags are breaking. The Hope, Faith, and Joy are slipping through my fingers.

But it isn't meant to be this way. I heard in a Sunday sermon that we are "hardwired for Hope." I like that saying. We as a people are certainly hopeful. But what are we hoping *for*?

The definition of HOPE is as follows :

hope/hōp/*noun*

a feeling of expectation and desire for a certain thing to happen. synonyms: aspiration, desire, wish, expectation, ambition, aim, goal, plan, design

(ARCHAIC)a feeling of trust.

"A desire for a certain thing to happen...." Perfect houses, perfect children, a perfect marriage, a perfect world? Yes, the whole Hallmark enchilada I could call my daily life. Did the second definition catch anyone's eye? It caught mine... *trust.* I took my research a step further and looked up the definition of "archaic." According to Oxford, it is as follows: "Archaic words: These words are no longer in everyday use or have lost a particular meaning in current usage"...Wow, I feel like I just cracked a serious code. The trust associated with the word Hope has "lost meaning." We sure do hope for things, but as in expecting and desiring **our** plans. But what if we anchored that Hope in His promises? His promises of *more.* Could we walk in faith knowing that when it all doesn't go perfectly according to our plan, it's still a perfect part of *His*? Friends, won't you give it a try? If we were to, ever so slightly, put down those heavy bags for a moment and reach out to accept His Heavenly help- hands wide open, eyes set high- can you imagine the possibilities?

～

There once was a man caught in a snowstorm. He hunkered down in his house and prayed that God would save him. There was a knock at the door, and it was a stranger driving a sleigh. The stranger told him to get in. But the man replied, "I'm waiting for my God to save me, I have Faith." So, the stranger left. The snowstorm continued.

There was another knock at the door. It was another stranger driving a sleigh. The stranger told the man to get in. But the man replied again, "I'm waiting for my God to save me, I have Faith." So, the stranger left.

As the snowstorm worsened, there was a pounding at the door. It was a third stranger driving a sleigh. The stranger asked the man to get in. But the man replied a third time. "I am waiting for my God to save me, I have Faith."

Well, folks, the man died in the snowstorm. And when he reached Heaven, he quickly asked God why He didn't save him. God calmly replied, "I sent you three sleighs...what else did you need?'

~

Did God send me a truck with a dashingly handsome driver to help scoop up my bruised ego and broken fingers?? Possibly. And probably. Does He continue to send these metaphorical "sleighs" each day, offering assistance and insights, many times without me even noticing? I'm 100% sure of it. My only suggestion now? When God sends you and me a sleigh or two, maybe we *might* want to push aside our foolishness and imagination on what we *think* we're waiting for and try reaching up, trusting where it's headed and stepping in.

After all, it's the only sleigh that can **truly and HOPE-FULL-y** <u>carry</u> it all.

THE STAIN MASTER

"As for me, I will always have Hope." - Psalm 71:14

DEFINITION: Messy

Webster's: "marked by confusion, disorder, or dirt... lacking neatness or precision."

My definition: proof of a beautiful, authentic, meaningful life being lived.

One morning while preparing for a new day with my darling Kindergarteners, I learned that big messes can be cleaned up by a little portion of grace with a side of humor. With minutes to spare until the beginning of school, hallways lined with energetic little ones, I ever so awkwardly tipped over a whole entire 5-pound jug of tiny colored beads from the top back shelf of my classroom closet. I will never forget the "whooshing" sound as they flooded the entire floor. That sound was followed by the bell, signaling the eager children to enter my room. I heard their sweet little voices filing in while talking about breakfast, shuffling chairs, and completely unaware of my absence. While inside the closet, I just stood, ankle-deep in the mess. I'll paint the picture again. Me- in the closet. 25 five-year olds - in the classroom. What on earth was I going to do? The crazy people in my head battled initially, urging me to hurry up and decide between cursing loudly or laughing hysterically. What came out of my mouth was a little bit of both. I started swearing the alphabet with tears. I went back and forth with my movements; at first walking quickly and thunderously, which surely gave away my hiding place and then sneaking, which only led to a redistribution of the plastic pieces with each pause like the tide coming in on a beach. I *wished* I were at the beach. I felt like I was stuck in the ball pit at Chuck E. Cheese. It took me so long to get through the mess, I made it all the way to the letter "F," covered in sweat. And, now, with the classroom suddenly silent on the other side of the door, I saw the handle *slowly* turning.

It seemed I had a choice to make. Should I wallow in my mistake, letting my day be weighed down by what went wrong? Or should I move forward with a little grace, walking out with a smile and leaving my mess behind? I'm happy to say I chose wisely. I trailed many beads throughout that epic day and, when I moved out years later, piles of beads were still spread across the closet floor.

Our days as mothers are full of these choices. Begin the day joyless or start with a sleepy smile and quick prayer? Make lunches with a groan or pack backpacks with a grateful heart? Snap at our husband while we pick up toys for the millionth time or mend with a hint of understanding? Get knocked down and stay down or reach up one more time? These decisions may seem small at first, but they add up. It's not just "one good decision leads to another," but one decision to open your heart makes way for another. And it's another moment closer to sweet surrender.

Looking back through the chronicles of my own scars and gazing into the continuous challenges, tests and cliff hanging, I truly believe that opening my hands, asking for help and surrendering is the opposite of weakness. I am grounded by knowing it's a strong step in the direction I'm meant to go. It is an action anchored in Hope, opening doors of promised joy to my motherhood and sprinkling peace in my messy life.

And it *will be* messy. Not all moments are as humorous or colorful as roller skating over a thousand beads. But as the pages of this book come to a close, I pray you see signs of hope threaded thoughtfully within the stories of failure and freedom.

Remember my white pinstriped couch I covered in red wine? After many washes, special solutions, and hours and hours of serious scrubbing, it's still not perfect. And I'm finally realizing it never will be. Those faded stains are now a slightly humorous reminder of how tottery and off-balance my life gets when I try to hold everything all at once in my tired hands.

And let us not forget that God is so much better than we are at this whole Life thing. He is a parent, a loving, Heavenly Father, so there's certainly going to be a huge learning curve. We're all going to fall flat, juggle, feel incredibly burdened or, at the very least, act like someone has pushed us out on the ice rink before we've even had time to tie our skates. But friends, that doesn't mean He's not with us.

The other day, after a wonderful afternoon playing in the creek down the street with my girls, God sent me another sleigh- and this one drove straight into my heart. Autumn and

Mattie had just caught tiny minnows with their bare hands and quickly bagged them to take home as pets (!) With their new treasures in plastic bubbles and somewhat nestled carefully between piles of soaked shorts and empty juice boxes, they each put on their backpacks. They looked up at me, unsure of how they would be able to carry the heavy load of gallon Ziplocs filled with creek water, pebbles, dirt, and new fishy friends. I turned them around, adjusted their straps while whispering to them both, "It's all about how you carry it. Try to stay with each other and I'm here if you need me." As we started off on the steamy trek home, I watched them proudly. The two sisters smiled at each other- hand in hand- walking slowly, in an exaggerated wedding march, sweetly careful and conscious of the priceless cargo slung over their backs. I pray I will never forget the sound of their contagious giggles and extravagant plans. It hit me then what God was saying: *I've given you someone. Many "someones." Friends...family...people...to aid you through this moment, this season. Look around, my precious child, and see them.*

Then there was Quinn. She had been unsuccessful at bare-handed-minnow-fishing (you have to sit *still* to achieve such a thing) and had decided to just bring large rocks home from the creek instead. I was thoroughly enjoying watching her as well. Walking boldly barefoot with rocks in one hand, crocs and an oversized leaf in the other, she never stopped singing her version of "If You're Happy And You Know It." She also never stopped trying to pick up things. With zero extra hands. At every intersection. I fought the instinct to liberate her, or scoop up all her various things to let her freely wander as she wished. No, I thought to myself. She wants the rocks, she's gotta carry them... And, boy, was it hard. But as we turned the last corner, I could see her sheer, stubborn grit and strength wearing thin. She was truly struggling and the rocks were slipping. She shouted, "Mooooooooommy!!" I immediately reached out and clasped her little hand in mine. I knelt down, looked into her wonder-filled green eyes and said, "You *can* hold them now, because now *I'm* holding *you...*"

It may seem like the burdens of life are unbearable. Like things are completely slipping out of our hands. God *is* allowing us to make those epic flubs, flops, and failures. He *is* allowing us to feel the weight, the same way a loving parent waits and watches silently in the wings as her child battles the words, "But I can't..." and you whisper to her, "But, darling, you *can*..." He also knows exactly *how much* we can. And the very second you can't go any further, calling out with surrender, your Heavenly Father steps in. When we "**D**o **I**t *with* **G**od," we are stronger and steadier than we ever imagined. Have no doubt that His unwavering hands are clasped around your precious life. Each and every morning, He longs for you and me to grow in these moments of motherhood as we learn the art of stretching and releasing, ultimately uncovering the best remedy of all for the millions of messes we've made.

So, the next time you're having the kind of day where you're scrubbing the counter or carpet with your hurting hands, take a moment of surrender and hold open one of those tired hands. Reach it up high. Higher still. Feel something pouring in from above. It's filling today's brokenness. It's healing your pain from the past. It's sending joy as you catch a glimpse of a brand new tomorrow. Close that beautiful hand and pull it close. There's something in there. It's always been there. But now, you know what it really is and you *have* it. My dear, sweet friends, it's *Hope*. Now, hold on tightly and never let it go. One day, I pray, you wake up and find there's nothing more perfect you'll need to carry with you.

"I have kicked up the dust and the dirt on the
     narrow road
I have had to let go of some hurt to hold on to hope
I've watched the sunset before the promise came
I have waded through waters wide and walked
     through the flame
And I can say

Every valley made me lift my eyes up
Every burden only made me stronger
Every sorrow only made Your joy go
Deeper and deeper, deeper, and deeper

I will run like I'm out to win, and finish the race
For every battle that's sure to come I will be brave
I've got my heart set on every word You say
And no matter what lies ahead You'll make a way..."-
     Deeper by Meredith Andrews

ABOUT THE AUTHOR

Monica Stoltzfus is an avid crafter, composer of words, coffee-addict, and chaos wrangler. Her debut picture book, The Ripple, received First place by the National Indie Excellence Awards for "Best Inspirational Children's Book". Her article about parenting during the pandemic appeared in the May '20 issue of Washington Magazine. When not writing, she can be found watching a Hallmark movie marathon, hunting for leaves on the streets, or most likely spilling something. She lives in Northern Virginia with her four fearless daughters and compassionate husband. (Yes, there's been a new baby since this book was written!) To stay updated on her journey of motherhood mayhem and faith-filled stories, check out her blog, www.justcomposeyourself.com.